PORTRAITS
AND
BIOGRAPHICAL
SKETCHES

The Secretaries of State

D1178258

For sale by the Superintendent of Documents, U.S. Government Printing Office
Washington, D.C. 20402

Stock Number 044-000-01708-3

DEPARTMENT OF STATE PUBLICATION 8921
Department and Foreign Service Series 162
Office of Public Communication
Bureau of Public Affairs

Released November 1978

Preface

This publication is a revision of one issued under the same title in 1956. Richard S. Patterson, then a member of the Department of State Historical Division, compiled the earlier version. The present, revised publication is the work of Lee H. Burke of the Office of the Historian and Jan K. Herman of the Office of Public Communication.

This edition covers the two Secretaries for Foreign Affairs and all the Secretaries of State. All except the last two Secretaries (Henry A. Kissinger and Cyrus R. Vance) are depicted by photographic reproductions of the Department of State collection of oil portraits. Although the collection has more than one portrait for some Secretaries, only one is included herein. Each reproduction is accompanied by a brief statement regarding the artist and the portrait. The information concerning the portrait collection that appeared in the preface of the 1956 edition now appears on page iv under the heading, "Note on the Department of State's Collection of Oil Portraits of the Secretaries of State."

Two of the original appendices ("Secretaries of State Ad Interim" and Chronological List of Presidents of the United States, Secretaries of State, and Secretaries of State Ad Interim") have been revised. One appendix ("Notes Regarding Other Oil Portraits Belonging to the Department of State") has been deleted.

Note on the Department of State's Collection of Oil Portraits of the Secretaries of State

The Department of State has gradually accumulated a collection of oil portraits of the former Secretaries of State. This collection is little known, however, and owing to the Department's lack of suitable space for its display it is not readily accessible.

The Department's collection of portraits includes a painting of each Secretary of State from Thomas Jefferson, who took office in 1790, to William P. Rogers. A portrait of Henry A. Kissinger is in preparation. For five of the Secretaries—Daniel Webster, Abel P. Upshur, John M. Clayton, William H. Seward, and William M. Evarts—the collection includes two portraits. In addition, there are portraits of the two Secretaries for Foreign Affairs, Robert R. Livingston and John Jay. The collection does not include portraits of Secretaries of State ad interim or Acting Secretaries of State, except in the case of Secretary ad interim Alvey A. Adee, of whom the Department possesses an oil portrait which it received as a gift.

The Department's collection of oil portraits of the Secretaries dates from 1861. Before retiring from office on March 5 of that year, Jeremiah S. Black, Secretary of State under President Buchanan, arranged for the purchase, from the artist John Pope, of a large portrait of Daniel Webster; the portrait was paid for on April 12, 1861.

Contents

Robert R. Livingston

ARTIST Stua

Robert R. Livingston

ROBERT R. LIVINGSTON was born in New York City, November 27, 1746; graduated from King's College (now Columbia) in 1765; married Mary Stevens in 1770; admitted to the bar the same year; member of the New York Provincial Convention 1775; delegate to the Continental Congress 1775—1776, 1779—1780, 1784—1785; served on several congressional committees, one being the committee to draft the Declaration of Independence; delegate to the New York State constitutional convention, 1777, and with Gouverneur Morris and John Jay drafted that state's constitution; helped secure New York's ratification of the Constitution in 1788; served as head of the Department of Foreign Affairs, the forerunner of the Department of State, 1781—1783; administered the presidential oath of office to George Washington in 1789; in 1801 became U.S. Minister to France; while there, helped effect the 1803 Louisiana Purchase; member of the New York Canal Commission in 1811; patron and partner of Robert Fulton; died at his estate in Clermont, New York, February 26, 1813.

Gilbert Stuart was born in North Kingston, Rhode Island, December 3, 1755; died in Boston, Massachusetts, July 9, 1828. This three-quarter length portrait of the seated Livingston was painted about 1790 and is on loan to the Department of State from the collection of Mr. John T. Wainwright. Size: 42 by 34 inches.

John Jay

ARTIST Conra

John Jay

JOHN JAY was born in New York City, December 12, 1745; graduated from King's College in 1764; admitted to the bar in 1768 and practiced law; married Sarah Van Brugh Livingston in 1774; member of the Continental Congress 1774—1779; as a member of the New York Provincial Congress in 1776—1777, aided in obtaining approval of the Declaration of Independence and in drafting the state constitution; Chief Justice of New York State 1777—1778; President of the Continental Congress 1778—1779; Minister to Spain 1779—1782; one of the Commissioners named in 1781 to negotiate peace with Great Britain, signed the treaties of 1782 and 1783; took office as Secretary for Foreign Affairs under the Continental Congress December 21, 1784, served until the establishment of government under the Constitution, and continued unofficially to superintend the Department until Jefferson took office as Secretary of State on March 22, 1790; during his tenure of office, treaties of commerce with Prussia and Morocco and a consular convention with France were negotiated; Chief Justice of the United States 1789—1795; Minister to Great Britain 1794—1795, negotiated and signed Jay's Treaty; Governor of New York 1795—1801; retired to his farm at Bedford, near New York City, where he died May 17, 1829.

Arthur S. Conrad (*originally Arthur E. Schmalz*) was born in Chicago, Illinois, February 8, 1907. His portrait of John Jay, which is a copy from paintings by Gilbert Stuart (1755—1828) and Joseph Wright (1756—1793), was done while he was an employee of the Department of State, 1947—1948. Inscription: "A. Conrad." An inscription on the back includes the following:

> Painted by A. Conrad in 1948 for the Department of State after portraits by Gilbert Stuart in the National Gallery and by Joseph Wright in the N.Y. Historical Society.

Size: 29¼ by 24½ inches.

C.L.Ransom.
after
Wilson Peale.

Thomas Jefferson

ARTIST Ranso

4

Thomas Jefferson

THOMAS JEFFERSON was born at "Shadwell," Goochland (now Albemarle) County, Virginia, April 13, 1743; graduated from the College of William and Mary in 1762; admitted to the bar and commenced practice in 1767; held various local public offices; member of the Virginia House of Burgesses 1769—1775; married Martha (Wayles) Skelton in 1772; member of the Continental Congress 1775—1776; prepared the first draft of the Declaration of Independence and signed the final Declaration; member of the Virginia House of Delegates 1776—1779; Governor of Virginia 1779—1781; again a member of the Continental Congress 1783—1784; one of three Ministers named in 1784 to negotiate treaties with European nations and the Barbary States; Minister to France 1785—1789; commissioned Secretary of State in President Washington's Cabinet September 26, 1789, entered upon his duties March 22, 1790, and served until December 31, 1793; as Secretary of State, successfully administered a policy of neutrality in the war between Great Britain and France; Vice President of the United States 1797—1801; President of the United States 1801—1809; retired to "Monticello," his estate in Virginia; engaged in literary, architectural, scientific, and agricultural pursuits; participated in the founding and served as rector of the University of Virginia; died at "Monticello," Albemarle County, Virginia, July 4, 1826.

Caroline L. Ormes Ransom was born in Newark, Ohio, in 1838; died in Washington, D.C. February 12, 1910. Her portrait of Thomas Jefferson is a copy of one which was painted from life in 1805 by Rembrandt Peale (1778—1860) and which is now owned by the New York Historical Society. The copy was purchased by the Department of State from Miss Ransom on July 15, 1881. Inscription: "C. L. Ransom. after Wilson [sic] Peale." Size: 27¼ by 22 inches.

Edmund Randolph

ARTIST Stapk

Edmund Randolph

EDMUND RANDOLPH was born at "Tazewell Hall," near Williamsburg, Virginia, August 10, 1753; attended the College of William and Mary; admitted to the bar and practiced in Williamsburg; appointed aide-de-camp to General Washington in 1775; member of the Virginia constitutional convention and Mayor of Williamsburg in 1776; married Elizabeth Nicholas the same year; Attorney General of Virginia 1776–1786; member of the Continental Congress 1779–1782; Governor of Virginia 1786–1788; delegate to the Annapolis Convention of 1786 and to the federal constitutional convention of 1787, member of the Virginia convention of 1788 that ratified the Constitution; member of the State House of Delegates 1788–1789; Attorney General in President Washington's Cabinet 1789–1794; commissioned Secretary of State January 2, 1794, entered upon his duties the same day, and served until August 20, 1795; as Secretary of State, directed the negotiation of the treaty of 1795 with Spain; moved to Richmond and resumed the practice of law; senior counsel for Aaron Burr in the treason trial of 1807; died in Clarke County, Virginia, September 12, 1813.

C. Gregory Stapko was born in Milwaukee, Wisconsin, March 14, 1913. His portrait of Edmund Randolph is a copy of one by Francis J. Fisher. This portrait, and also portraits of James Monroe and Edward Livingston, were painted in March—May 1949 and were purchased by the Department of State from Mr. Stapko on June 2, 1949. No inscription on the face. An inscription on the back reads: "Copy painted from original in State Capitol Richmond, Va. by C. G. Stapko of Edmund Randolph by Francis J. Fisher. Order No. 9301—49." Size: 28¼ by 23½ inches.

Timothy Pickering

ARTIST Conrad

8

Timothy Pickering

TIMOTHY PICKERING was born in Salem, Massachusetts, July 17, 1745; graduated from Harvard College in 1763; admitted to the bar in 1768 and commenced practice in Salem; held various local public offices; entered the Revolutionary Army as a colonel in 1775; elected to the State Legislature in 1776; married Rebecca White the same year; appointed Adjutant General and elected by the Continental Congress as a member of the Board of War in 1777; Quartermaster General of the Army 1780–1785; entered mercantile business in Philadelphia in 1785; organized Luzerne County, Pennsylvania, and represented it in the convention of 1787 that ratified the federal Constitution and in the state constitutional convention of 1789–1790; Postmaster General 1791–1795; Secretary of War in President Washington's Cabinet in 1795; Secretary of State ad interim August 20–December 9, 1795; commissioned Secretary of State December 10, 1795, entered upon his duties the same day, and served until May 12, 1800, when he was dismissed from office; as Secretary of State, opposed the French in the "X Y Z Affair" of 1797–1798 and entered into preparations for war; became Chief Justice of the Massachusetts Court of Common Pleas in 1802; Senator from Massachusetts 1803–1811; member of the State Executive Council 1812–1813; Representative from Massachusetts 1813–1817; died in Salem, January 29, 1829.

Arthur S. Conrad painted also the Department's portrait of John Jay (*q.v.*) and one of the two portraits of William M. Evarts. His portrait of Timothy Pickering, which is a copy of one by Gilbert Stuart (1755–1828), was painted while Mr. Conrad was an employee of the Department of State, 1947–1948. Inscription: "A. Conrad." An inscription on the back includes the following: "after the portrait painted in 1808 by Gilbert Stuart and owned by Miss Rebecca Pickering Thomas of Jamaica Plain, Mass. Painted by Arthur Conrad in 1948 for the Department of State." Size: 29¼ by 24½ inches.

John Marshall

ARTISTAndrew

10

John Marshall

JOHN MARSHALL was born near Germantown, in what became Fauquier County, Virginia, September 24, 1755; privately educated; officer in the Revolution; studied law at the College of William and Mary, admitted to the bar in 1780, and began practice; member of the Virginia Assembly 1782—1791 and 1795—1797; member of the state Executive Council 1782—1784; married Mary Willis Ambler in 1783; member of the Virginia convention of 1788 that ratified the federal Constitution; one of the "X Y Z" commissioners of 1797—1798 to adjust differences with France; Representative from Virginia 1799—1800; commissioned Secretary of State in President Adams' Cabinet May 13, 1800, entered upon his duties June 6, 1800, and served until February 4, 1801; as Secretary of State, directed the negotiation of the reconciliation convention of 1800 with France; commissioned Chief Justice of the United States January 31, 1801, and took office February 4, 1801; continued as Secretary of State ad interim February 4—March 4, 1801; member of the Virginia constitutional convention of 1829; author of a five-volume biography of George Washington; during thirty-four years as Chief Justice of the United States, established the authority and prestige of the Supreme Court; died in Philadelphia, Pennsylvania, July 6, 1835.

Eliphalet Fraser Andrews was born in Steubenville, Ohio, June 11, 1835; died in Washington, D.C., March 19, 1915. His portrait of John Marshall, which is a copy of one by Henry Inman (1801—1846), was purchased by the Department of State from Mr. Andrews on November 25, 1891. Inscription: "E. F. Andrews 1891 After Inman." Size: 29½ by 24¼ inches.

James Madison

ARTIST Heaton

James Madison

JAMES MADISON was born at Port Conway, Virginia, March 16, 1751; graduated from the College of New Jersey in 1771; studied law and admitted to the bar; elected to the Virginia constitutional convention and member of the state Assembly in 1776; member of the state Executive Council 1778—1779; member of the Continental Congress 1780—1783 and 1786—1788; Virginia House of Delegates 1784—1786; delegate to the Annapolis convention of 1786 and to the federal convention of 1787, where he played a major part in the framing of the Constitution; cooperated with Hamilton and Jay on a series of essays later published as *The Federalist*; member of the Virginia convention of 1788 that ratified the Constitution; Representative from Virginia 1789—1797; married Dolly (Payne) Todd in 1794; again a member of the House of Delegates in 1799; served as presidential elector in 1800; commissioned Secretary of State in President Jefferson's Cabinet March 5, 1801, entered upon his duties May 2, 1801, and served until March 3, 1809; during his tenure of office France offered and the United States accepted the Louisiana Purchase; President of the United States 1809—1817; retired to "Montpellier" (now "Montpelier"), his estate in Virginia; became rector of the University of Virginia in 1826; member of the Virginia constitutional convention of 1829; died at "Montpellier," Orange County, Virginia, June 28, 1836.

Augustus Goodyear Heaton was born in Philadelphia, Pennsylvania, April 28, 1844; died in Washington, D.C., October 11, 1930. His portrait of James Madison is a copy of one which was painted from life in 1816 by John Vanderlyn (1775—1852) and which is now owned by the James Monroe Law Office, Fredericksburg, Virginia. The copy was purchased by the Department of State from Mr. Heaton on December 21, 1891. Inscription: "A. G. Heaton Wash 1891." Size: 29½ by 24¼ inches.

Robert Smith

ARTIST Thorp

Robert Smith

ROBERT SMITH was born in Lancaster, Pennsylvania, November 3, 1757; moved with his parents to Baltimore, Maryland, at an early age; graduated from the College of New Jersey in 1781; served briefly as a private in the Continental Army; studied law, admitted to the bar in Baltimore, and soon had a large admiralty practice; one of the presidential electors of Maryland in 1789; married Margaret Smith in 1790; member of the Maryland Senate 1793—1795, and of the House of Delegates 1796—1800; sat in the Baltimore city council 1798—1801; served as Secretary of the Navy in President Jefferson's Cabinet 1801—1809; nominated, confirmed, and commissioned Attorney General in 1805, but did not serve; commissioned Secretary of State in President Madison's Cabinet March 6, 1809, entered upon his duties the same day, and served until April 1, 1811; as Secretary of State, negotiated the Smith-Erskine Agreement of 1809, rejection of which by the British Government marked a turning point in the relations between the two countries; returned to Baltimore, where he filled offices in various private organizations; died in Baltimore, November 26, 1842.

Freeman Thorp was born in Geneva, Ohio, June 16, 1844; died in Hubert, Minnesota, October 20, 1922. His portrait of Robert Smith, which is a copy, was purchased by the Department of State from Mr. Thorp on April 9, 1902. Inscription: "Thorp 1902." Size: 35 by 28¼ inches.

James Monroe

ARTIST Stapko

16

James Monroe

JAMES MONROE was born in Westmoreland County, Virginia, April 28, 1758; attended the College of William and Mary 1774—1776; officer in the Continental Army; studied law under Jefferson 1780—1783; member of the Virginia Assembly in 1782 and 1786; member of the Continental Congress 1783—1786; attended the Annapolis convention of 1786; married Eliza Kortright the same year; admitted to the bar and practiced in Fredericksburg; member of the state convention of 1788 that ratified the federal Constitution; Senator from Virginia 1790—1794; Minister to France 1794—1796; Governor of Virginia 1799—1802; again Minister to France in 1803; served as Minister to Great Britain 1803—1807; headed a diplomatic mission to Spain 1804—1805; again elected to the Virginia Assembly in 1810; again Governor of Virginia in 1811; commissioned Secretary of State in President Madison's Cabinet April 2, 1811, entered upon his duties April 6, 1811, and served until September 30, 1814; both Secretary of War and Secretary of State ad interim October 1, 1814—February 28, 1815; again commissioned Secretary of State February 28, 1815, entered upon his duties the same day, and served until March 3, 1817; during his tenure of office the War of 1812 was fought and the Treaty of Ghent, which restored peace, was negotiated; President of the United States 1817—1825; retired to his farm in Virginia; presiding officer of the Virginia constitutional convention of 1829; died in New York City, July 4, 1831.

C. Gregory Stapko painted also the Department's portraits of Edmund Randolph (*q.v.*) and Edward Livingston. His portrait of James Monroe is a copy of one by John Vanderlyn (1775—1852). The three portraits were painted in March—May 1949 and were purchased by the Department of State from Mr. Stapko on June 2, 1949. No inscription on the face. An inscription on the back reads: "Copy painted from original in National Gallery of Art—Wash. D.C. by C. G. Stapko of James Monroe by Vanderlyn Order No. 9301—49." Size: 28¼ by 23½ inches.

John Quincy Adams

ARTIST Gibert

John Quincy Adams

JOHN QUINCY ADAMS was born in Braintree (now Quincy), Massachusetts, July 11, 1767; studied in France and the Netherlands; served briefly as private secretary to the American Minister to Russia in 1781; secretary to his father during the peace negotiations with Great Britain 1782–1783; graduated from Harvard University in 1787; admitted to the bar in 1790 and practiced in Boston; served as Minister Resident to the Netherlands 1794–1797; married Louisa Catherine Johnson in 1797; Minister to Prussia 1797–1801; elected to the Massachusetts Senate in 1802; Senator from Massachusetts 1803–1808; professor of rhetoric and oratory at Harvard 1806–1809; Minister to Russia 1809–1814; head of the commission that negotiated the Treaty of Ghent with Great Britain in 1814; Minister to Great Britain 1815–1817; commissioned Secretary of State in President Monroe's Cabinet March 5, 1817, entered upon his duties September 22, 1817, and served until March 3, 1825; as Secretary of State, negotiated the treaty of 1819 with Spain for the cession of the Floridas and collaborated with the President in the formulation of the Monroe Doctrine; President of the United States 1825–1829; Representative from Massachusetts 1831–1848; author of many writings and speeches and a notable diary covering half a century; died in Washington, D.C., February 23, 1848.

Jean-Baptiste-Adolphe Gibert was born in Pointe-à-Pitre, Guadeloupe, January 24, 1803; lived for several years in Washington, D.C.; died, probably in Rome, Italy, in 1889. His portrait of John Quincy Adams is thought to have been painted from life. It came into the possession of Mrs. Columbus Munroe, daughter of William Winston Seaton (1785–1866), editor of the Washington *National Intelligencer*, and was purchased by the Department of State from her son, Seaton Munroe, on January 24, 1891. No inscription. Size: 26 x 21 inches.

Henry Clay

ARTIST Marchant

Henry Clay

HENRY CLAY was born in Hanover County, Virginia, April 12, 1777; attended public school; studied law in Richmond, Virginia; admitted to the bar and commenced practice in Lexington, Kentucky, in 1797; married Lucretia Hart in 1799; served in the state House of Representatives 1803–1806; Senator from Kentucky 1806–1807; served again in the state House of Representatives 1807–1809; again Senator from Kentucky 1810–1811; Representative from Kentucky and Speaker of the House 1811–1814; one of the Commissioners who negotiated the Treaty of Ghent with Great Britain in 1814; again Representative from Kentucky 1815–1821 and 1823–1825, and Speaker of the House 1815–1820 and 1823–1825; unsuccessful candidate for the presidency in 1824; commissioned Secretary of State in President John Quincy Adams' Cabinet March 7, 1825, entered upon his duties the same day, and served until March 3, 1829; as Secretary of State, negotiated a number of commercial treaties and sought unsuccessfully to have the United States participate in the Inter-American Congress at Panama in 1826; again Senator from Kentucky 1831–1842; Whig candidate for the Presidency in 1832 and in 1844; in retirement 1845–1848; again Senator from Kentucky 1849–1852; died in Washington, D.C., June 29, 1852.

Edward Dalton Marchant was born in Edgartown, Massachusetts, December 16, 1806; died in Asbury Park, New Jersey, August 15, 1887. His portrait of Henry Clay was painted from life in 1838. It was purchased by the Department of State, together with a portrait of John Quincy Adams which is no longer in the Department, from the artist's widow and daughter on September 29, 1890, for the sum of $2,500 ($1,250 for each portrait), this amount having been made available for the purpose by an act of Congress approved August 30, 1890. With a letter to the Department dated September 20, 1890, the artist's daughter, Adeline B. Marchant, enclosed the following statement:

While passing the summer of 1838 in Cincinnati, Mr. Marchant, who was an intense admirer of Mr. Clay, conceived the idea of adding his portrait to a collection he was engaged in making for himself, of the distinguished men of our own country. Accordingly, being armed with letters from prominent men, one of which, I believe, was from Hon. Thos. Ewing, he went to Ashland [Clay's home, near Lexington, Ky.], where he was kindly received by Mr. Clay, who at once acceded to his request, & insisted upon his making his home with him during the progress of the picture. After completing the head, &c. which occupied about ten days, he returned to Cincinnati where he finished the drapery. The picture was seen by a number of persons at Mr. Clay's own house, and was applauded without a dissenting voice, Mrs. Clay actually shedding tears over it. She was anxious to retain it, but Mr. Marchant felt that he must have the original, and offered to make her a copy, but this she refused, saying that it was the best ever painted of him, & she was afraid the copy would not suit her as well.

Inscription: "E D Marchant 1838." Size: 29¼ by 24¼ inches.

Martin Van Buren

ARTIST Andrew

Martin Van Buren

MARTIN VAN BUREN was born at Kinderhook, near Albany, New York, December 5, 1782; attended local schools; admitted to the bar and commenced practice in Kinderhook in 1803; married Hannah Hoes in 1807; moved to Hudson, New York, where he was surrogate 1808–1813; served in the state Senate 1812–1820; chosen regent of the University of New York in 1815; state Attorney General 1816–1819, residing in Albany; delegate to the state constitutional convention of 1821; Senator from New York 1821–1828; Governor of New York in 1829; commissioned Secretary of State in President Jackson's Cabinet March 6, 1829, entered upon his duties March 28, 1829, and served until May 23, 1831; as Secretary of State, settled a long-standing dispute with Great Britain over West Indian trade and obtained important treaties with Turkey and France; served as Minister to Great Britain 1831–1832 on a recess appointment that failed confirmation by the Senate; Vice President of the United States 1833–1837; President of the United States 1837–1841; unsuccessful candidate for the presidency on the Democratic ticket in 1840 and on the Free-soil ticket in 1848; retired to "Lindenwald," his country home at Kinderhook, New York, where he died July 24, 1862.

Eliphalet Fraser Andrews also painted the Department's portraits of John Marshall (*q.v.*) and James Buchanan and one of two portraits of Abel P. Upshur. His portrait of Martin Van Buren, which is a copy of one by George Peter Alexander Healy (1813–1894), was purchased by the Department of State from Mr. Andrews on November 25, 1891. Inscription: "E. F. Andrews After H[ealy] 1891." Size: 29¼ by 24 inches.

Edward Livingston

ARTIST Stapk

Edward Livingston

EDWARD LIVINGSTON was born at "Clermont," Columbia County, New York, May 28, 1764; graduated from the College of New Jersey in 1781; admitted to the bar in 1785 and practiced in New York City; married Mary McEvers in 1788 (died 1801); Representative from New York 1795—1801; United States Attorney for the District of New York and Mayor of New York City 1801—1803; moved to New Orleans in 1804 and practiced law; married Louise Moreau de Lassy (née D'Avezac) in 1805; aide to General Jackson at the Battle of New Orleans; elected to the Louisiana House of Representatives in 1820; prepared a penal code for the state which, though not adopted, brought him fame; engaged in a protracted controversy with the federal government over title to land known as Batture Sainte Marie, which was finally decided in his favor; Representative from Louisiana 1823—1829; Senator from Louisiana 1829—1831; commissioned Secretary of State in President Jackson's Cabinet May 24, 1831, entered upon his duties the same day, and served until May 29, 1833; as Secretary of State, drafted the celebrated Nullification Proclamation of 1832; Minister to France 1833—1835; died at "Montgomery Place," Dutchess County, New York, May 23, 1836.

C. Gregory Stapko also painted the Department's portraits of Edmund Randolph (q.v.) and James Monroe. His portrait of Edward Livingston is a copy of one by John Trumbull (1756—1843). The three portraits were painted in March—May 1949 and were purchased by the Department of State from Mr. Stapko on June 2, 1949. No inscription on the face. An inscription on the back reads: "Copy painted from original in City Hall New York by C. G. Stapko of Edward Livingston by John Trumbull Ord. No. 9301—49." Size: 28 by 23¼ inches.

Louis McLane

Louis McLane

LOUIS McLANE was born in Smyrna, Delaware, May 28, 1786; midshipman in the Navy 1798—1801; attended Newark Academy (now the University of Delaware); admitted to the bar in 1807 and commenced practice in Smyrna; married Catherine Mary Milligan in 1812; served in the War of 1812; Representative from Delaware 1817—1827; Senator from Delaware 1827—1829; Minister to Great Britain 1829—1831; Secretary of the Treasury in President Jackson's Cabinet 1831—1833; commissioned Secretary of State May 29, 1833, entered upon his duties the same day, and served until June 30, 1834; as Secretary of State, reorganized the Department, introducing systematic procedure into its operations; became president of the Morris Canal & Banking Company in New York City; moved to Baltimore, Maryland, where he was president of the Baltimore & Ohio Railroad Company 1837—1847; while holding the last-mentioned position, again Minister to Great Britain 1845—1846; delegate to the Maryland constitutional convention of 1850; died in Baltimore, October 7, 1857.

Robert Hinckley was born in Boston, Massachusetts, April 3, 1853; died in Rehoboth Beach, Delaware, June 1, 1941. His portrait of Louis McLane, which is a copy, was purchased by the Department of State from Mr. Hinckley on July 28, 1891. Inscription: "Robert Hinckley." Size: 29 by 24 inches.

John Forsyth

ARTIST Tho

John Forsyth

JOHN FORSYTH was born in Fredericksburg, Virginia, October 22, 1780; moved to Augusta, Georgia, with his parents; graduated from the College of New Jersey in 1799; admitted to the bar in 1802 and commenced practice in Augusta; married Clara Meigs in 1801 or 1802; became Attorney General of Georgia in 1808; Representative from Georgia 1813—1818; Senator from Georgia 1818—1819; Minister to Spain 1819—1823; again Representative from Georgia 1823—1827; Governor of Georgia 1827—1829; again Senator from Georgia 1829—1834; delegate to the anti-tariff convention at Milledgeville, Georgia, in 1832; earned the reputation of being one of the most powerful debaters of his time; commissioned Secretary of State in President Jackson's Cabinet June 27, 1834, entered upon his duties July 1, 1834, continued in office under President Van Buren, and served until March 3, 1841; as Secretary of State, brought to a successful conclusion a serious controversy with France regarding payment under the claims convention of 1831; died in Washington, D.C., October 21, 1841.

Freeman Thorp also painted the Department's portrait of Robert Smith *(q.v.)*. His portrait of John Forsyth, which is a copy, was purchased by the Department of State from Mr. Thorp on March 6, 1890. Inscription: "Thorp 1890" in two places. Size: 29 by 24¼ inches.

Daniel Webster

Daniel Webster

DANIEL WEBSTER was born in Salisbury, New Hampshire, January 18, 1782; graduated from Dartmouth College in 1801; taught school; admitted to the bar in 1805 and commenced practice in Boscawen, New Hampshire; moved to Portsmouth, New Hampshire, in 1807; married Grace Fletcher in 1808 (died 1828); Representative from New Hampshire 1813—1817; moved to Boston in 1816 and soon became known as one of the foremost lawyers and orators of his time; presidential elector in 1820; delegate to the Massachusetts constitutional convention of 1820—1821; member of the state House of Representatives in 1822; Representative from Massachusetts 1823—1827; Senator from Massachusetts 1827—1841; married Caroline Le Roy in 1829; was nominated by the state legislature for the presidency in 1836; commissioned Secretary of State in President Harrison's Cabinet March 5, 1841 entered upon his duties March 6, 1841, continued in office under President Tyler, and served until May 8, 1843; as Secretary of State, negotiated the famous Webster-Ashburton Treaty of 1842 with Great Britain; again Senator from Massachusetts 1845—1850; commissioned Secretary of State in President Fillmore's Cabinet July 22, 1850, entered upon his duties July 23, 1850, and served until his death in Marshfield, Massachusetts, October 24, 1852.

George Peter Alexander Healy was born in Boston, Massachusetts, July 15, 1813; died in Chicago, Illinois, June 24, 1894. His portrait of Daniel Webster, painted in 1848, is a replica of one which he painted from life in 1842 and which is now owned by the New-York Historical Society. This replica, together with a portrait of Lord Ashburton by the same artist, was purchased from Mrs. Daniel Webster by the congressional Joint Committee on the Library of Congress in 1879 out of an appropriation for "Works of Art for the Capitol," the sum of $3,000 being paid for each portrait. On December 30, 1879, Senator Daniel W. Voorhees, on behalf of the Joint Committee, requested the Department of State to place these portraits in its diplomatic reception room, and on January 5, 1880, the Department replied that it would be pleased to do so. No inscription. A plaque attached to the frame reads: "Painted by G. P. A. Healy—1848." Size: 49 by 39 inches.

Abel Parker Upshur

ARTIST Heaton

Abel Parker Upshur

ABEL PARKER UPSHUR was born at "Vaucluse," Northampton County, Virginia, June 17, 1791; attended the College of New Jersey and Yale College; admitted to the bar in 1810 and practiced in Richmond; member of the Virginia House of Delegates 1812–1813 and 1825–1827; married Elizabeth Dennis, who died; married Elizabeth A. B. Upshur in 1826; judge of the General Court of Virginia 1826–1829; delegate to the State constitutional convention of 1829; judge of the reorganized General Court 1830–1841; Secretary of the Navy in President Tyler's Cabinet 1841–1843; served as Secretary of State ad interim June 24–July 23, 1843; commissioned Secretary of State July 24, 1843, entered upon his duties the same day, and served until his death; as Secretary of State, reopened negotiations for the annexation of Texas; killed by the explosion of a gun aboard the U.S. warship *Princeton* on the Potomac River about fifteen miles below Washington, D.C., February 28, 1844.

Augustus Goodyear Heaton also painted the Department's portrait of James Madison (*q.v.*). His portrait of Abel P. Upshur, which is a copy, was purchased by the Department of State from Mr. Heaton on July 30, 1892. Inscription: "A. G. Heaton Wash. 92." Size: 29 by 24¼ inches.

John Caldwell Calhoun

ARTIST Barney

John Caldwell Calhoun

JOHN CALDWELL CALHOUN was born at "the Long Canes settlement," in what became Abbeville County, South Carolina, March 18, 1782; graduated from Yale College in 1804 and from Litchfield Law School in 1806; admitted to the bar in 1807 and commenced practice in Abbeville, South Carolina; married Floride Bonneau Colhoun in 1811; gave up the practice of law and established himself as a planter; member of the state House of Representatives 1808—1809; Representative from South Carolina 1811—1817; Secretary of War in President Monroe's Cabinet 1817—1825; Vice President of the United States 1825—1832, when he resigned; Senator from South Carolina 1832—1843; commissioned Secretary of State in President Tyler's Cabinet March 6, 1844, entered upon his duties April 1, 1844, and served until March 10, 1845; as Secretary of State, signed an abortive treaty for the annexation of Texas and aided in accomplishing annexation by joint resolution of Congress; delegate of South Carolina to, and presiding officer of, a railroad-and-waterway convention held in Memphis, Tennessee, in 1845; again Senator from South Carolina 1845—1850; author of voluminous writings and speeches; died in Washington, D.C., March 31, 1850.

Alice (Pike) Barney was born in Cincinnati, Ohio, January 14, 1860; died in Los Angeles, California, October 12, 1931. Her portrait of John C. Calhoun, which is a copy, was purchased by the Department of State from Mrs. Barney on July 30, 1892. Inscription: "Alice Barney." Size: 28¼ by 22¾ inches.

James Buchanan

ARTIST Andrew

James Buchanan

JAMES BUCHANAN was born at Cove Gap, near Mercersburg, Pennsylvania, April 23, 1791; graduated from Dickinson College in 1809; admitted to the bar in 1812 and practiced in Lancaster, Pennsylvania; served in the defense of Baltimore in the War of 1812; member of the Pennsylvania House of Representatives 1814—1816; Representative from Pennsylvania 1821—1831; Minister to Russia 1832—1833; Senator from Pennsylvania 1834—1845; commissioned Secretary of State in President Polk's Cabinet March 6, 1845, entered upon his duties March 10, 1845, and served until March 7, 1849; as Secretary of State, negotiated and signed the Oregon Treaty of 1846 with Great Britain, directed the negotiation of the Treaty of Guadalupe Hidalgo of 1848 with Mexico, and sought unsuccessfully to purchase Cuba from Spain; unsuccessful candidate for the Democratic presidential nomination in 1852; served as Minister to Great Britain 1853—1856; one of the three United States Ministers who drew up the "Ostend Manifesto" of 1854; President of the United States 1857—1861; retired to "Wheatland," his country estate near Lancaster; never married; died at "Wheatland" June 1, 1868.

Eliphalet Fraser Andrews also painted the Department's portraits of John Marshall *(q.v.)* and Martin Van Buren and one of the two portraits of Abel P. Upshur. His portrait of James Buchanan, which is a copy of one by George Peter Alexander Healy (1813—1894), was purchased by the Department of State from Mr. Andrews on February 8, 1893. Inscription: "E. F. Andrews. Aft. Healy, 1892." Size: 29 by 24 inches.

John Middleton Clayton

ARTIST Hinckley

John Middleton Clayton

JOHN MIDDLETON CLAYTON was born at Dagsboro, Sussex County, Delaware, July 24, 1796; graduated from Yale College in 1815; attended Litchfield Law School; admitted to the bar in 1819, commenced practice in Dover, Delaware, and won a reputation unrivaled in the state; married Sarah Ann Fisher in 1822; member of the state House of Representatives 1824—1826; Secretary of State of Delaware 1826—1828; Senator from Delaware 1829—1836; delegate to the state constitutional convention of 1831; Chief Justice of Delaware 1837—1839; engaged in scientific farming near New Castle, Delaware, and gained a wide reputation as an agriculturist; again Senator from Delaware 1845—1849; commissioned Secretary of State in President Taylor's Cabinet March 7, 1849, entered upon his duties March 8, 1849, and served until July 22, 1850; as Secretary of State, negotiated and signed the Clayton-Bulwer Treaty of 1850 with Great Britain; resumed his agricultural pursuits; again Senator from Delaware 1853—1856; died in Dover, November 9, 1856.

Robert Hinckley also painted the Department's portraits of Louis McLane (*q.v.*), Edward Everett, William L. Marcy, and Alvey A. Adee. His portrait of John M. Clayton, which is a copy, was purchased by the Department of State from Mr. Hinckley on July 28, 1891. Inscription: "Robert Hinckley." Size: 29 by 24¼ inches.

Daniel Webster

ARTIST Pope

Daniel Webster

DANIEL WEBSTER, who served previously as Secretary of State under Presidents Harrison and Tyler, 1841 —1843, commissioned Secretary of State in President Fillmore's Cabinet July 22, 1850, entered upon his duties July 23, 1850, and continued in office until his death on October 24, 1852. A biographical sketch appears on page 33.

John Pope was born in Gardiner, Maine, in 1821; died in New York City December 29, 1880. His portrait of Daniel Webster, although listed in the Department's *Catalogue* of 1900 as a copy, may have been painted from life in Boston, Massachusetts, about 1850. This portrait was ordered by Secretary of State Jeremiah S. Black and was purchased by the Department of State from Mr. Pope on April 12, 1861. Inscription: "J Pope." Size: 50 by 38 inches.

Edward Everett

ARTIST Hinckle

Edward Everett

EDWARD EVERETT was born in Dorchester, Massachusetts, April 11, 1794; graduated from Harvard University in 1811; pursued theological studies and received his M.A. degree in 1814; became pastor of the Brattle Street Unitarian Church, Boston, in 1814; studied and traveled in Europe 1815—1819, receiving his Ph.D. degree at Göttingen in 1817; occupied the chair of Greek literature at Harvard 1819—1825; edited the *North American Review* 1820—1824; married Charlotte Gray Brooks in 1822; Representative from Massachusetts 1825—1835; Governor of Massachusetts 1836—1839; Minister to Great Britain 1841—1845; president of Harvard 1846—1849; commissioned Secretary of State in President Fillmore's Cabinet November 6, 1852, entered upon his duties the same day, and served until March 3, 1853; as Secretary of State, declined a proposal of France and Great Britain that the United States enter into a convention with them guaranteeing to Spain the possession of Cuba; Senator from Massachusetts 1853—1854; became known as one of the greatest orators of his day; unsuccessful candidate for the Vice Presidency on the Constitutional Union ticket in 1860; presidential elector in 1864; died in Boston, January 15, 1865.

Robert Hinckley also painted the Department's portraits of Louis McLane (*q.v.*), John M. Clayton, William L. Marcy, and Alvey A. Adee. His portrait of Edward Everett, which is a copy, was purchased by the Department of State from Mr. Hinckley on August 13, 1888. No inscription. Size: 29 by 24¼ inches.

William Learned Marcy

ARTIST Hinckle

William Learned Marcy

WILLIAM LEARNED MARCY was born in Sturbridge (now Southbridge), Massachusetts, December 12, 1786; graduated from Brown University in 1808; admitted to the bar in 1811 and commenced practice in Troy, New York; married Dolly Newell in 1812 (died 1821); served in the War of 1812; recorder of Troy 1816—1818 and 1821—1823; became Adjutant General of New York in 1821; state Comptroller 1823—1829; married Cornelia Knower about 1825; Associate Justice of the state Supreme Court 1829—1831; Senator from New York 1831—1833; Governor of New York 1833—1838; member of the Mexican Claims Commission 1840—1842; Secretary of War in President Polk's Cabinet 1845—1849; resumed the practice of law; commissioned Secretary of State in President Pierce's Cabinet March 7, 1853, entered upon his duties March 8, 1853, and served until March 6, 1857; as Secretary of State, negotiated or directed the negotiation of numerous treaties, among them the Gadsden Treaty of 1853 with Mexico and the reciprocity treaty of 1854 with Great Britain, and settled various delicate problems of international relations, among them the Koszta case with Austria, the *Black Warrior* case with Spain, and the Patrice Dillon case with France; died at Ballston Spa, New York, July 4, 1857.

Robert Hinckley also painted the Department's portraits of Louis McLane (*q.v.*), John M. Clayton, Edward Everett. His portrait of William L. Marcy, which is a copy, was purchased by the Department of State from Mr. Hinckley on December 10, 1891. No inscription. Size: 29 by 24¼ inches.

Lewis Cass

Lewis Cass

LEWIS CASS was born in Exeter, New Hampshire, October 9, 1782; attended Exeter Academy; went to the Northwest Territory in 1799; admitted to the bar in 1802 and practiced in Zanesville, Ohio; married Elizabeth Spencer in 1806; elected to the Ohio House of Representatives the same year; United States Marshal for the District of Ohio 1807—1812; served with distinction in the War of 1812, attaining the rank of brigadier general; Governor of Michigan Territory 1813—1831; Secretary of War in President Jackson's Cabinet 1831—1836; served as Minister to France 1836—1842; unsuccessful candidate for the Democratic presidential nomination in 1844 and again in 1852; Senator from Michigan 1845—1848; was the Democratic candidate for the Presidency in 1848; again Senator from Michigan 1849—1857; commissioned Secretary of State in President Buchanan's Cabinet March 6, 1857, entered upon his duties the same day, and served until December 14, 1860; as Secretary of State, obtained British acceptance of the American construction of the Clayton-Bulwer Treaty and abandonment by Great Britain of its claim to a right to visit and search American vessels; returned to his home in Detroit, Michigan, and engaged in literary pursuits; died in Detroit, June 17, 1866.

The artist who painted the Department's portrait of Lewis Cass has not been identified, and no record of the date or manner of acquisition of the portrait by the Department of State has been found. Evidently it was not in the Department in 1900, for it is not mentioned in the *Catalogue* of that year; but it is listed in a memorandum dated July 1, 1931. No inscription. Size: 49¼ by 35½ inches.

Jeremiah Sullivan Black

Jeremiah Sullivan Black

JEREMIAH SULLIVAN BLACK was born near Stony Creek, Somerset County, Pennsylvania, January 10, 1810; attended public schools; admitted to the bar in 1830 and began the practice of law; appointed Deputy Attorney General of Somerset County in 1831; married Mary Forward in 1836; served as President Judge of the Court of Common Pleas for the sixteenth judicial district 1842—1851; elected to the state Supreme Court in 1851 and was reelected in 1854, by lot serving the first three years as Chief Justice; served as Attorney General in President Buchanan's Cabinet 1857—1860; commissioned Secretary of State December 17, 1860, entered upon his duties the same day, and served until March 5, 1861; as Secretary of State, instructed the principal United States representatives in Europe to use their best efforts to prevent recognition of the Confederate States; appointed United States Supreme Court reporter in 1861 and prepared *Black's Reports*, in two volumes; moved to York, Pennsylvania, and resumed the practice of law; engaged in controversial writing; member of the Pennsylvania constitutional convention of 1872—1873; counsel for William Belknap in his impeachment trial in 1876 and for Samuel J. Tilden before the Electoral Commission in 1877; died in York, August 19, 1883.

Walter Manton was born in Rhode Island; was a clerk in the Treasury Department 1881—1882 and a clerk in the Department of State 1882—1895. His portrait of Jeremiah S. Black, which is a copy, was purchased by the Department of State from Mr. Manton on November 18, 1891. Inscription: "W. Manton." Size: 29¼ by 24¼ inches.

William Henry Seward

ARTIST Brady

William Henry Seward

WILLIAM HENRY SEWARD was born at Florida, Orange County, New York, May 16, 1801; graduated from Union College in 1820; admitted to the bar in 1822 and commenced practice in Auburn, New York, in 1823; married Frances Miller in 1824; member of the State Senate 1830—1834; Governor of New York 1838—1842; resumed the practice of law; Senator from New York 1849—1861; unsuccessful candidate for the Republican presidential nomination in 1860; commissioned Secretary of State in President Lincoln's Cabinet March 5, 1861, entered upon his duties March 6, 1861, continued in office under President Johnson, and served until March 4, 1869; as Secretary of State, handled with skill the delicate relations of the United States with foreign nations during the Civil War, and in 1867 negotiated and signed the treaty with Russia for the cession of Alaska to the United States; made a trip around the world 1870—1871 and was everywhere accorded an enthusiastic reception; retired to his home in Auburn in 1871, where he died October 10, 1872.

Mathew B. Brady was born in Warren County, New York, about 1823; died in New York City, January 15, 1896. His portrait of William H. Seward is an example of a Brady method of using in combination the arts of photography and oil portraiture. Based on an enlargement of a Brady photograph, the portrait was finished in oils. The brushwork was probably done not by Mr. Brady himself, but by one or another of several artists whom he employed from time to time for such work. According to an inventory of Mr. Brady's effects dated April 1873, this portrait was then on display in the reception room of the Brady Gallery in Washington. It was purchased by the Department of State from Mr. Brady on August 3, 1878. In a letter to the Department dated May 24, 1878, Mr. Brady wrote:

> . . . This portrait is considered the most perfect likeness of the celebrated original, taken from life in this city [Washington], in the full fruition of his genius and great national renown, at a time fraught with great danger to this Republic! It has always been considered a standard likeness and extensively copied in Europe and this country for the purpose of engraving and lithographing . . . .

Frederick William Seward, son of William H. Seward and Assistant Secretary of State 1861—1869 and 1877—1879, wrote to the Department on January 11, 1898:

> Mr. Brady made several photographs of my father. But one, taken just before or during the War, was considered the best likeness, and proved to be the one most satisfactory to the public. It was often copied and reproduced, and used for engravings and illustrations.
>
> I have been under the impression—possibly a mistaken one—that Mr. Brady had this photograph enlarged and made the basis of the portrait which the Department afterwards purchased from him.—I do not remember to have heard the name of the artist who painted it,—but his work was certainly done with spirit and skill . . . .

No inscription. Size: 29 by 24¼ inches.

Elihu Benjamin Washburne

ARTIST Hea

Elihu Benjamin Washburne

ELIHU BENJAMIN WASHBURNE was born in Livermore, Maine, September 23, 1816; attended the common schools; held an editorial position on the Augusta *Kennebec Journal*; attended Harvard Law School in 1839 and was admitted to the Massachusetts bar in 1840; moved to Galena, Illinois, later the same year and commenced the practice of law; delegate to the Whig National Conventions at Baltimore in 1844 and 1852; married Adèle Gratiot in 1845; Representative from Illinois 1853—1869; commissioned Secretary of State in President Grant's Cabinet March 5, 1869, entered upon his duties the same day, and served until March 16, 1869, a period of only twelve days; served as Minister to France 1869—1877 and was the only official representative of a foreign government to remain in Paris during the siege of 1870—1871 and the days of the Commune; on his return to the United States, settled in Chicago, Illinois, and engaged in historical and literary pursuits; unsuccessful candidate for the Republican presidential nomination in 1880; president of the Chicago Historical Society 1884—1887; died in Chicago October 22, 1887.

George Peter Alexander Healy also painted one of the Department's two portraits of Daniel Webster (see pp. 32—33). His portrait of Elihu B. Washburne is thought to have been done from life. It came into possession of the Department of State sometime between 1883 and 1900, but no record has been found of the date or manner of its acquisition. Inscription: "G. P. A. Healy. Chicago, August, 21st 1883." Size: 45¼ by 34½ inches.

Hamilton Fish

ARTIST Huntington

Hamilton Fish

HAMILTON FISH was born in New York City, August 3, 1808; graduated from Columbia College in 1827; admitted to the bar in 1830 and practiced in New York City; married Julia Kean in 1836; Representative from New York 1843–1845; Lieutenant Governor of New York in 1848 and Governor 1849–1850; Senator from New York 1851–1857; president general of the Society of the Cincinnati 1854–1893; during the Civil War, on a Board of Commissioners of the federal government for the relief and exchange of prisoners; president of the New-York Historical Society 1867–1869; commissioned Secretary of State in President Grant's Cabinet March 11, 1869, entered upon his duties March 17, 1869, and served until March 12, 1877; as Secretary of State, was one of the Commissioners of the United States who negotiated the Treaty of Washington of 1871 with Great Britain for the settlement of differences between the two countries, directed negotiations that resulted in the settlement of American claims against Spain, and signed the reciprocity treaty of 1875 with Hawaii; retired from public life; died at "Glen Clyffe," his estate near Garrison, New York, September 7, 1893.

Daniel Huntington was born in New York City, October 14, 1816; died in New York City, April 18, 1906. His portrait of Hamilton Fish, which is thought to have been done from life, was purchased by the Department of State from Mr. Huntington on December 23, 1881. Inscription: "D. Huntington 1881." Size: 29 by 24¼ inches.

William Maxwell Evarts

ARTIST Conrad

William Maxwell Evarts

WILLIAM MAXWELL EVARTS was born in Boston, Massachusetts, February 6, 1818; graduated from Yale College in 1837; attended Harvard Law School 1838—1839; admitted to the bar in 1841 and practiced in New York City; married Helen Minerva Wardner in 1843; Assistant United States Attorney for the Southern District of New York 1849—1853; chairman of the New York delegation to the Republican National Convention at Chicago in 1860; member of a government mission to Great Britain 1863—1864; delegate to the New York State constitutional convention of 1867—1868; chief counsel for President Johnson in the impeachment trial of 1868; Attorney General in President Johnson's Cabinet 1868—1869; one of counsel for the United States before the tribunal of arbitration at Geneva 1871—1872; chief counsel for the Republican Party before the Electoral Commission in 1877; commissioned Secretary of State in President Hayes' Cabinet March 12, 1877, entered upon his duties the same day, and served until March 7, 1881; as Secretary of State, defined American policy with regard to an isthmian canal, took a strong stand toward Mexico in defense of American lives and property, and directed the negotiation of treaties with China relating to commerce and immigration; delegate to the International Monetary Conference at Paris in 1881; Senator from New York 1885—1891; died in New York City, February 28, 1901.

Arthur S. Conrad also painted the Department's portraits of John Jay (*q.v.*) and Timothy Pickering. His portrait of William M. Evarts, which is a copy from a photograph, was painted while Mr. Conrad was an employee of the Department of State, 1947—1948. Inscription: "A. Conrad 1948." An inscription on the back includes the following: "Painted from a photograph in 1948 for the Department of State by Arthur Conrad." Size: 29¼ by 24¾ inches.

James Gillespie Blaine

James Gillespie Blaine

JAMES GILLESPIE BLAINE was born in West Brownsville, Pennsylvania, January 31, 1830; graduated from Washington College in 1847; taught school in Kentucky; married Harriet Stanwood in 1850; taught school and studied law in Philadelphia 1852—1854; moved in 1854 to Maine, where he purchased an interest in the Augusta *Kennebec Journal* and served on the editorial staff of the Portland *Advertiser*; one of the founders of the Republican Party; member of the Maine House of Representatives 1859—1862 and Speaker of the House 1861—1862; served as chairman of the Republican State Committee 1859—1881; Representative from Maine 1863—1876 and Speaker of the House 1869—1875; Senator from Maine 1876—1881; unsuccessful candidate for the Republican presidential nomination in 1876 and again in 1880; commissioned Secretary of State in President Garfield's Cabinet March 5, 1881, entered upon his duties March 7, 1881, continued in office under President Arthur, and served until December 19, 1881; Republican candidate for the Presidency in 1884; commissioned Secretary of State in President Harrison's Cabinet March 5, 1889, entered upon his duties March 7, 1889, and served until June 4, 1892; as Secretary of State, convened and presided over the First Pan American Conference in 1889; died in Washington, D.C., January 27, 1893.

James Archer was born in Edinburgh, Scotland, June 10, 1823; visited the United States and Canada 1884—1887; died at Shian, Haslemere, Surrey, England, September 3, 1904. His portrait of James G. Blaine, which was painted from life in 1885, was purchased by the Department of State from Mr. Archer on February 6, 1885. Inscription: "JA" monogram and "1885." Size: 47¼ by 36¾ inches.

Frederick Theodore Frelinghuysen

ARTIST Huntingto

Frederick Theodore Frelinghuysen

FREDERICK THEODORE FRELINGHUYSEN was born in Millstone, New Jersey, August 4, 1817; graduated from Rutgers College in 1836; admitted to the bar in 1839 and practiced in Newark, New Jersey; married Matilde E. Griswold in 1842; city attorney of Newark in 1849 and a member of the city council in 1850; trustee of Rutgers College 1851—1885; representative of New Jersey at the peace congress held in Washington, D.C., early in 1861; Attorney General of New Jersey 1861—1866; Senator from New Jersey 1866—1869 and 1871—1877; member of the Electoral Commission of 1877 to decide the contested presidential election of 1876; resumed the practice of law; commissioned Secretary of State in President Arthur's Cabinet December 12, 1881, entered upon his duties December 19, 1881, and served until March 6, 1885; as Secretary of State, fostered commercial relations with Latin America, sent delegates to the Berlin Conference of 1884—1885 on the Congo, and opened treaty relations with Korea; died in Newark, May 20, 1885.

Daniel Huntington also painted the Department's portrait of Hamilton Fish (*q.v.*). His portrait of Frederick T. Frelinghuysen was purchased by the Department of State from Mr. Huntington on July 16, 1885, after Mr. Frelinghuysen's death. Inscription: "D. Huntington 1885." Size: 29 by 24 inches.

Thomas Francis Bayard

ARTIST Whitma

Thomas Francis Bayard

THOMAS FRANCIS BAYARD was born in Wilmington, Delaware, October 29, 1828; attended private schools and an academy at Flushing, New York; studied law, was admitted to the bar in 1851, and commenced practice in Wilmington; United States District Attorney for Delaware 1853—1854; moved to Philadelphia, Pennsylvania, and practiced law there, returning to Wilmington in 1858; married Louise Lee in 1856 (died 1886); Senator from Delaware 1869—1885; member of the Electoral Commission of 1877 to decide the contested presidential election of 1876; unsuccessful candidate for the Democratic presidential nomination in 1876, in 1880, and again in 1884; commissioned Secretary of State in President Cleveland's Cabinet March 6, 1885, entered upon his duties March 7, 1885, and served until March 6, 1889; as Secretary of State, paved the way for settlement of the Samoan question with Great Britain and Germany, arranged a solution regarding fisheries that allayed difficulties with Canada, and upheld the special interest of the United States in the Hawaiian Islands; resumed the practice of law in Wilmington; married Mary W. Clymer in 1889; served as Ambassador to Great Britain 1893—1897; died in Dedham, Massachusetts, September 28, 1898.

Sarah de St. Prix (Wyman) Whitman was born in Baltimore, Maryland, in 1842; died in Boston, Massachusetts, June 24, 1904. Her portrait of Thomas F. Bayard, which is thought to have been done from life, was purchased by the Department of State from Mrs. Whitman on February 10, 1893. Inscription: "MDC SW CCXCII," the initials SW being within an acorn-shaped figure. Size: 55 by 36¼ inches.

John Watson Foster

ARTIST Floy

John Watson Foster

JOHN WATSON FOSTER was born in Pike County, Indiana, March 2, 1836; graduated from Indiana University in 1855 (A.M. 1858); attended Harvard Law School; admitted to the bar in 1857 and commenced practice in Evansville, Indiana; married Mary Parke McFerson in 1859; served in the Union Army, attaining the rank of brevet brigadier general; edited the Evansville *Daily Journal* 1865—1869 and postmaster of Evansville 1869—1873; chairman of the Republican State Committee in 1872; Minister to Mexico 1873—1880 and Minister to Russia 1880—1881; established an international law practice in Washington, D.C.; Minister to Spain 1883—1885; special plenipotentiary to negotiate reciprocity agreements 1890—1891; agent of the United States in the Fur-seal Arbitration 1892—1893; commissioned Secretary of State in President Harrison's Cabinet June 29, 1892, entered upon his duties the same day, and served until February 23, 1893; as Secretary of State signed the abortive treaty of 1893 for the annexation of Hawaii; Commissioner for China in the negotiation of the treaty of peace of 1895 with Japan; Ambassador on special mission to Great Britain and Russia in 1897; agent of the United States before the Alaska Boundary Tribunal in 1903; represented China at the Second Hague Conference in 1907; author of numerous published writings; died in Washington, November 15, 1917.

Henry Floyd (*originally Harry Floyd*) was born in London, England; resided in Washington, D.C. about 1895—1904; died after 1912. His portrait of John W. Foster, which is thought to have been done from life, was purchased by the Department of State from Secretary of State John Hay on May 11, 1900. This portrait is said to have been "substituted for another one by a different artist." Inscription: "Henry Floyd. 1899." Size: 42¼ by 32¼ inches.

Walter Quintin Gresham

ARTIST Pebble

Walter Quintin Gresham

WALTER QUINTIN GRESHAM was born near Lanesville, Harrison County, Indiana, March 17, 1832; attended Indiana University; admitted to the bar in 1854 and practiced in Corydon, Indiana; married Matilda McGrain in 1858; elected to the state Legislature in 1860; served in the Union Army, attaining the rank of brevet major general of volunteers; opened a law office in New Albany, Indiana, in 1865; financial agent of Indiana in New York City 1867–1869; delegate to the Republican National Convention at Chicago in 1868; United States Judge for the District of Indiana 1869–1883; Postmaster General in President Arthur's Cabinet 1883–1884 and Secretary of the Treasury briefly in 1884; United States Circuit Judge for the Seventh Judicial District 1884–1893; unsuccessful candidate for the Republican presidential nomination in 1888; went over to the Democratic Party in 1892; commissioned Secretary of State in President Cleveland's Cabinet March 6, 1893, entered upon his duties March 7, 1893, and served until his death; as Secretary of State, advised against resubmission to the Senate of the annexation treaty of 1893 with Hawaii, and brought about the settlement of a dispute between Great Britain and Nicaragua; died in Washington, D.C., May 28, 1895.

Francis Marion Pebbles was born in Wethersfield, Wyoming County, New York, October 16, 1839; died in Alameda, California, December 2, 1928. His portrait of Walter Q. Gresham is perhaps a replica of a portrait by Mr. Pebbles which Mrs. Gresham presented to the Emperor of Japan. It was purchased by the Department of State from Mr. Pebbles on October 7, 1895, after Mr. Gresham's death. Inscription: "Frank M. Pebbles 1895." Size: 54¼ by 41¾ inches.

Richard Olney

ARTIST Vo

Richard Olney

RICHARD OLNEY was born in Oxford, Massachusetts, September 15, 1835; graduated from Brown University in 1856 (A.M.) and from Harvard Law School in 1858; admitted to the bar in 1859 and commenced practice in Boston, Massachusetts; married Agnes Park Thomas in 1861; member of the Massachusetts House of Representatives in 1874; Attorney General in President Cleveland's Cabinet 1893—1895; commissioned Secretary of State June 8, 1895, entered upon his duties June 10, 1895, and served until March 5, 1897; as Secretary of State, induced the British Government to submit to arbitration its dispute with Venezuela over the boundary between Venezuela and British Guiana, and insisted on the protection of American lives and property and on reparation for injuries in the disorders then prevailing in Cuba, China, and Turkey; resumed the practice of law; regent of the Smithsonian Institution 1900—1908; American member of the Permanent International Commission under the Bryan-Jusserand Treaty of 1914 with France 1915—1917; died in Boston, April 8, 1917.

Hubert Vos was born in Maastricht, Netherlands, February 17, 1855; came to the United States in 1892 and was naturalized in 1898; died in New York City, January 8, 1935. His portrait of Richard Olney, which was painted from life in Boston, Massachusetts, in 1897, was purchased by the Department of State from Mr. Olney on October 9, 1897. Inscription: "Hubert Vos 97." Size: 45 by 35¾ inches.

John Sherman

ARTIST Whippl

John Sherman

JOHN SHERMAN was born in Lancaster, Ohio, May 10, 1823; attended a local academy; admitted to the bar in 1844 and practiced in Mansfield, Ohio; married Margaret Sarah Cecilia Stewart in 1848; delegate to the Whig National Conventions of 1848 and 1852; moved to Cleveland, Ohio, in 1853; chairman of the first Republican convention in Ohio in 1855 and participated in the organization of the national Republican Party; Representative from Ohio 1855—1861; Senator from Ohio 1861—1877; Secretary of the Treasury in President Hayes' Cabinet 1877—1881; again Senator from Ohio 1881—1897; authority on matters of federal finance; unsuccessful candidate for the Republican presidential nomination in 1880, in 1884, and again in 1888; commissioned Secretary of State in President McKinley's Cabinet March 5, 1897, entered upon his duties March 6, 1897, and served until April 27, 1898; as Secretary of State, supported the American interpretation of most-favored-nation treatment in matters relating to international trade; retired from public life; died in Washington, D.C., October 22, 1900.

Charles Ayer Whipple was born in Southboro, Massachusetts, in 1859; died in Washington, D.C., May 2, 1928. His portrait of John Sherman, which is thought to have been done from life, was purchased by the Department of State from Mr. Whipple on July 7, 1898. Inscription: "C. Ayer Whipple. 1896." Size: 51 by 39½ inches.

William Rufus Day

ARTIST Rosentha

72

William Rufus Day

WILLIAM RUFUS DAY was born in Ravenna, Ohio, April 17, 1849; graduated from the University of Michigan in 1870; admitted to the bar in 1872 and commenced practice in Canton, Ohio; married Mary Elizabeth Schaefer in 1875; Judge of the Court of Common Pleas 1886—1890; appointed United States Judge for the Northern District of Ohio in 1889, but because of ill health resigned before taking office; served as Assistant Secretary of State 1897—1898; commissioned Secretary of State in President McKinley's Cabinet April 26, 1898, entered upon his duties April 28, 1898, and served until September 16, 1898; as Secretary of State, secured the neutrality of the nations of western Europe in the Spanish-American War and signed the protocol of 1898 for the cessation of hostilities; chairman of the United States Commission that negotiated and signed the treaty of peace of 1898 with Spain; Judge of the United States Court of Appeals for the Sixth Circuit 1899—1903; Associate Justice of the United States Supreme Court 1903—1922; Umpire in the Mixed Claims Commission, United States and Germany, 1922—1923; died at his summer home at Mackinac Island, Michigan, July 9, 1923.

Albert Rosenthal was born in Philadelphia, Pennsylvania, January 30, 1863; died in New York City December 20, 1939. His portrait of William R. Day, painted from life in 1903, was purchased by the Department of State from Mr. Rosenthal on January 18, 1904. This disbursement was the subject of a congressional investigation in 1911. Inscription: "Albert Rosenthal 1903." An inscription on the back includes the information that the portrait was painted in Washington, D.C., in October—November 1903. Size: 39½ by 29½ inches.

John Hay

John Hay

JOHN HAY was born in Salem, Indiana, October 8, 1838; graduated from Brown University in 1858; admitted to the Illinois bar in 1861; private secretary to President Lincoln 1861—1865; Secretary of Legation at Paris 1865—1867, Chargé d'Affaires ad interim at Vienna 1867—1868, and Secretary of Legation at Madrid 1869—1870; journalist with the New York *Tribune* 1870—1875; engaged successfully in the writing of verse and fiction; married Clara Louise Stone in 1874; Assistant Secretary of State 1879—1881; made frequent trips to Europe 1881—1896; co-author with John G. Nicolay of *Abraham Lincoln: A History* (10 volumes, 1890); Ambassador to Great Britain 1897—1898; commissioned Secretary of State in President McKinley's Cabinet September 20, 1898, entered upon his duties September 30, 1898, continued in office under President Roosevelt, and served until his death; as Secretary of State, supported the "open door" policy in China, prevented the dissolution of the Chinese Empire in 1900, obtained settlement of the Alaska-Canada boundary controversy, acquired a clear title to Tutuila, and secured by treaty the right for the United States to construct and defend the Panama Canal; died at his summer home at Newbury, New Hampshire, July 1, 1905.

Ellen G. Emmet *(later Mrs. William Blanchard Rand)* was born in San Francisco, California, March 4, 1876; died in New York City December 18, 1941. Her portrait of John Hay was purchased by the Department of State from Miss Emmet on July 20, 1906, after Mr. Hay's death.

In December 1907, at Mrs. Hay's request, the portrait was temporarily removed from the Department to enable the artist to make certain alterations in it. No inscription. Size: 49½ by 38¼ inches.

Elihu Root

ARTIST Emmet

Elihu Root

ELIHU ROOT was born in Clinton, New York, February 15, 1845; graduated from Hamilton College in 1864 and from New York University Law School in 1867; admitted to the bar in 1867 and practiced in New York City; married Clara Frances Wales in 1878; United States Attorney for the Southern District of New York 1883—1885; delegate to the state constitutional convention of 1894; Secretary of War in the Cabinets of Presidents McKinley and Roosevelt 1899—1904; member of the Alaskan Boundary Tribunal in 1903; commissioned Secretary of State in President Roosevelt's Cabinet July 7, 1905, entered upon his duties July 19, 1905, and served until January 27, 1909; as Secretary of State, created the American-Canadian International Joint Commission and negotiated arbitration treaties with twenty-four nations; Senator from New York 1909—1915; was counsel for the United States in the North Atlantic Coast Fisheries Arbitration in 1910; became a member of the Permanent Court of Arbitration the same year; president of the Carnegie Endowment for International Peace 1910—1925; president of the New York State constitutional convention of 1915; chief of a special mission to Russia in 1917; member of the committee of jurists which planned the Permanent Court of International Justice in 1920; delegate to the Washington Conference on Limitation of Armament 1921—1922; died in New York City, February 7, 1937.

Ellen G. Emmet also painted the Department's portraits of John Hay (*q.v.*) and Henry L. Stimson. Her portrait of Elihu Root, which was painted from life in 1907, was substituted by Secretary of State Philander C. Knox for a portrait of Mr. Root by George Benjamin Luks (1867—1933). The Luks portrait was purchased by the Department of State from the artist on July 6, 1909. No record has been found of the date or other circumstances of its replacement with the Emmet portrait. Inscription: "Ellen Emmet 1907." Size: 49½ by 39½ inches.

Robert Bacon

ARTIST Sorolla

Robert Bacon

ROBERT BACON was born in Jamaica Plain, Massachusetts, July 5, 1860; graduated from Harvard University in 1880; after a trip around the world, commenced a business career with Lee, Higginson & Company of Boston in 1881; married Martha Waldron Cowdin in 1883; member of the firm of E. Rollins Morse & Brother of Boston 1883—1894; member of the New York firm of J. P. Morgan & Company 1894—1903; Assistant Secretary of State 1905—1909 and Acting Secretary while Elihu Root was in South America in 1906; commissioned Secretary of State in President Roosevelt's Cabinet January 27, 1909, entered upon his duties the same day, and served until March 5, 1909; as Secretary of State, obtained the advice and consent of the Senate to the canal treaties of 1909 with Colombia and Panama; Ambassador to France 1909—1912; became a Fellow of Harvard in 1912; made a journey to South America at the request of the Carnegie Endowment for International Peace in 1913; went to France in August 1914 and helped with the work of the "American Ambulance"; commissioned a major and detailed to General Pershing's staff in 1917; promoted to lieutenant colonel in 1918 and served as Chief of the American Military Mission at British General Headquarters; died in New York City, May 29, 1919.

Joaquin Sorolla y Bastida was born in Valencia, Spain, February 27, 1863; visited the United States in 1909; died in Cercedillo, a suburb of Madrid, Spain, August 10, 1923. His portrait of Robert Bacon, which was painted from life in New York City in 1909, was presented to the Department of State by Mr. Bacon in October 1909. Inscription: "J Sorolla y Bastida N.Y. 1909." Size: 43¾ by 33¾ inches.

Philander Chase Knox

ARTIST Jongers

Philander Chase Knox

PHILANDER CHASE KNOX was born in Brownsville, Pennsylvania, May 6, 1853; graduated from Mount Union College in 1872; admitted to the bar in 1875 and practiced in Pittsburgh, Pennsylvania; Assistant United States Attorney for the Western District of Pennsylvania 1876—1877; married Lillie Smith in 1880; president of the Pennsylvania Bar Association in 1897; as counsel for the Carnegie Steel Company, took a prominent part in organizing the United States Steel Corporation in 1901; Attorney General in the Cabinets of Presidents McKinley and Roosevelt 1901—1904; Senator from Pennsylvania 1904—1909; unsuccessful candidate for the Republican presidential nomination in 1908; commissioned Secretary of State in President Taft's Cabinet March 5, 1909, entered upon his duties March 6, 1909, and served until March 5, 1913; as Secretary of State, reorganized the Department on a divisional basis, extended the merit system to the Diplomatic Service up to the grade of chief of mission, pursued a policy of encouraging and protecting American investments abroad, and accomplished the settlement of the Bering Sea controversy and the North Atlantic fisheries controversy; resumed the practice of law in Pittsburgh; again Senator from Pennsylvania 1917—1921; died in Washington, D.C., October 12, 1921.

Alphonse Jongers was born in Mézières, France, November 17, 1872; resided in Montreal, Canada, and New York City; died in Montreal, October 2, 1945. His portrait of Philander C. Knox, which is thought to have been done from life, was purchased by the Department of State from Mr. Jongers on January 30, 1913. Inscription: "Alphonse Jongers—1913." Size: 55¼ by 41¼ inches.

William Jennings Bryan

ARTIST Wiles

William Jennings Bryan

WILLIAM JENNINGS BRYAN was born in Salem, Illinois, March 19, 1860; graduated from Illinois College in 1881 (A.M. 1884) and from Union College of Law in 1883; admitted to the bar in 1883 and practiced in Jacksonville, Illinois; married Mary Elizabeth Baird in 1884; moved to Lincoln, Nebraska, in 1887 and continued the practice of law; delegate to the Democratic state convention in 1888; Representative from Nebraska 1891—1895; edited the Omaha *World-Herald* 1894—1896; delegate to the Democratic national conventions in 1896, 1904, 1912, 1920, and 1924; Democratic candidate for the Presidency in 1896, in 1900, and again in 1908; raised a regiment of volunteer infantry in 1898 and was commissioned colonel; founded a weekly newspaper, *The Commoner,* in 1901; toured the world 1905—1906; engaged in editorial writing and delivering Chautauqua lectures; commissioned Secretary of State in President Wilson's Cabinet March 5, 1913, entered upon his duties the same day, and served until June 9, 1915; as Secretary of State, negotiated treaties "for the advancement of peace" with thirty nations; resumed his writing and lecturing; established his home in Miami, Florida, in 1921; opposed Clarence Darrow as counsel in the Scopes trial at Dayton, Tennessee, in 1925; died in Dayton, July 26, 1925.

Irving Ramsay Wiles was born in Utica, New York, April 8, 1861; died July 29, 1948. His portrait of William Jennings Bryan, which was painted from life in New York City in November 1916, was purchased by the Department of State from Mr. Wiles on March 10, 1917. Inscription: "Irving R. Wiles 1917." Size: 59¼ by 39½ inches.

Robert Lansing

Robert Lansing

ROBERT LANSING was born in Watertown, New York, October 17, 1864; graduated from Amherst College in 1886; admitted to the bar in 1889 and practiced in Watertown; married Eleanor Foster in 1890; associate counsel for the United States in the Bering Sea Arbitration 1892—1893; counsel for the Mexican and Chinese Legations in Washington 1894—1895 and 1900—1901; counsel for the United States before the Bering Sea Claims Commission 1896—1897, before the Alaskan Boundary Tribunal in 1903, in the North Atlantic Coast Fisheries Arbitration 1908—1910, and in the American and British Claims Arbitration in 1912; agent of the United States in the last-mentioned arbitration 1913—1914; instrumental in founding the American Society of International Law in 1906 and in establishing the *American Journal of International Law* in 1907; Counselor of the Department of State 1914—1915; Secretary of State ad interim June 9—23, 1915; commissioned Secretary of State in President Wilson's Cabinet June 23, 1915, entered upon his duties June 24, 1915, and served until February 13, 1920; as Secretary of State, protested against British blockade and contraband practices, and signed the treaty of 1916 for the purchase of the Danish West Indies and the Lansing-Ishii Agreement of 1917 with Japan; practiced international law in Washington, D.C.; died in Washington, October 30, 1928.

Philip Alexius de László de Lombos (*originally Fülöp Elek von László*) was born in or near Budapest, Hungary, April 28, 1869; moved to London, England, in 1907 and became a naturalized British subject in 1914; died in Hampstead, London, November 22, 1937.

His portrait of Robert Lansing, which is thought to have been done from life, was purchased by the Department of State on March 13, 1921 but the Department's records do not now show from whom the purchase was made. Inscription: "de László 1921." Size: 35¼ by 23¼ inches.

Bainbridge Colby

ARTIST Vol

Bainbridge Colby

BAINBRIDGE COLBY was born in St. Louis, Missouri, December 22, 1869; graduated from Williams College in 1890 and from New York Law School in 1892; admitted to the bar and practiced in New York City; married Nathalie Sedgwick in 1895 (divorced 1929); member of the state Assembly 1901-1902; assisted in founding the Progressive Party and was a delegate to its conventions in 1912 and 1916; counsel for a joint committee of the New York Legislature in an investigation of the public-utility commissions and public-service corporations in 1916; special assistant to the United States Attorney General in anti-trust proceedings in 1917; member of the American Mission to the Inter-Allied Conference at Paris the same year; member of the United States Shipping Board 1917–1919 and a trustee and vice president of the Emergency Fleet Corporation in 1918; commissioned Secretary of State in President Wilson's Cabinet March 22, 1920, entered upon his duties March 23, 1920, and served until March 4, 1921; as Secretary of State, forcefully enunciated American policy toward Soviet Russia and toward the mandates over former German colonies; practiced law in partnership with Woodrow Wilson in New York City 1921–1923; continued the practice of law; married Anne (von Ahlstrand) Ely in 1929; died in Bemus Point, New York, April 11, 1950.

Stephen Arnold Douglas Volk was born in Pittsfield, Massachusetts, February 23, 1856; died in Fryeburg, Maine, February 7, 1935. His portrait of Bainbridge Colby, which was painted from life in New York City in 1922–1923, was purchased by the Department of State from Mr. Colby on May 19, 1923. Inscription: "Douglas Volk." Size: 39¼ by 31½ inches.

Charles Evans Hughes

Charles Evans Hughes

CHARLES EVANS HUGHES was born in Glens Falls, New York, April 11, 1862; graduated from Brown University in 1881 (A.M. 1884) and from Columbia Law School in 1884; admitted to the bar in 1884 and practiced in New York City; married Antoinette Carter in 1888; professor of law at Cornell University 1891—1893; counsel for committees of the New York Legislature 1905—1906; special assistant to the United States Attorney General in the coal investigation in 1906; Governor of New York 1907—1910; Associate Justice of the United States Supreme Court 1910—1916; Republican candidate for the presidency in 1916; commissioned Secretary of State in President Harding's Cabinet March 4, 1921, entered upon his duties March 5, 1921, continued in office under President Coolidge, and served until March 4, 1925; as Secretary of State, presided over the Washington Conference on Limitation of Armament 1921—1922; member of the Permanent Court of Arbitration 1926—1930; chairman of the United States delegation to the Sixth Pan American Conference in 1928 and delegate to the Pan American Conference on Arbitration and Conciliation 1928—1929; judge of the Permanent Court of International Justice 1928—1930; Chief Justice of the United States Supreme Court 1930—1941; died in Osterville, Massachusetts, August 27, 1948.

Howard Chandler Christy was born in Morgan County, Ohio, January 10, 1873; died in New York City, March 3, 1952. His portrait of Charles E. Hughes, which was painted from life in 1924, was presented to the Department of State by Colonel William Eric Fowler, of Washington, D.C., at a simple ceremony held at noon on March 18, 1925, in what was then known as "the large diplomatic reception room". Inscription: "Howard Chandler Christy 1924." Size: 55 by 39¾ inches.

Frank Billings Kellogg

ARTIST de Lászl

Frank Billings Kellogg

FRANK BILLINGS KELLOGG was born in Potsdam, New York, December 22, 1856; went to Minnesota with his parents 1865; attended public schools; admitted to the bar in 1877 and commenced practice in Rochester, Minnesota; City Attorney of Rochester 1878—1881 and Olmsted County attorney 1882—1887; married Clara Margaret Cook in 1886; moved to St. Paul, Minnesota, in 1887 and continued the practice of law; Government delegate to the Universal Congress of Lawyers and Jurists at St. Louis, Missouri, in 1904; member of the Republican National Committee 1904—1912 and a delegate to the Republican National Conventions in 1904, 1908, and 1912; special counsel for the government to prosecute anti-trust suits; president of the American Bar Association 1912—1913; Senator from Minnesota 1917—1923; delegate to the Fifth Pan American Conference in 1923; served as Ambassador to Great Britain 1923—1925; commissioned Secretary of State in President Coolidge's Cabinet February 16, 1925, entered upon his duties March 5, 1925, and served until March 28, 1929; as Secretary of State, was co-author of the Kellogg-Briand Peace Pact of 1928; awarded the Nobel Peace Prize in 1929; resumed the practice of law in St. Paul; judge of the Permanent Court of International Justice 1930—1935; died in St. Paul, December 21, 1937.

Philip Alexius de László de Lombos painted also the Department's portrait of Robert Lansing (*q.v.*). His portrait of Frank B. Kellogg, which is dated 1931, is evidently a replica or a version of one which was painted from life in London in the latter half of April 1929. It was presented to the Department of State by Mr. Kellogg on a date now unknown but prior to May 17, 1933. Inscription: "de László 1931. XII. W." Size: 39½ by 32¼ inches.

Henry Lewis Stimson

ARTIST Rand

Henry Lewis Stimson

HENRY LEWIS STIMSON was born in New York City, September 21, 1867; graduated from Yale University in 1888; attended Harvard University (A.M. 1889) and Harvard Law School 1889—1890; admitted to the bar in 1891 and practiced in New York City; married Mabel Wellington White in 1893; United States Attorney for the Southern District of New York 1906—1909; Secretary of War in President Taft's Cabinet 1911—1913; delegate at large to the New York State constitutional convention of 1915; served in the United States Army in France 1917—1918, attaining the rank of colonel; practiced law in New York City; special representative of the President to Nicaragua in 1927; Governor General of the Philippine Islands 1927—1929; commissioned Secretary of State in President Hoover's Cabinet March 5, 1929, entered upon his duties March 28, 1929, and served until March 4, 1933; as Secretary of State, was chairman of the American delegation to the London Naval Conference in 1930, and formulated the "Stimson Doctrine" with regard to Japanese activities in China; resumed the practice of law in New York City; Secretary of War in the Cabinets of Presidents Roosevelt and Truman 1940—1945; retired from public life; died at "Highhold," his estate in West Hills, Huntington Township, Long Island, October 20, 1950.

Ellen (Emmet) Rand also painted the Department's portraits of John Hay (*q.v.*) and Elihu Root. Her portrait of Henry L. Stimson was painted from life in 1933 for Mr. Stimson, who had it sent to the Department of State in October 1933 on the understanding that it was to "be treated temporarily as a loan." It was received in the Department on October 25 and was hung in Secretary of State Cordell Hull's anteroom the following day. The loan developed eventually into a gift. Inscription:"Ellen Emmet Rand 1933." Size: 42¾ by 33 inches.

Cordell Hull

ARTIST Murr

Cordell Hull

CORDELL HULL was born in Overton (now Pickett) County, Tennessee, October 2, 1871; attended National Normal University, Lebanon, Ohio, 1889—1890; delegate to the Tennessee Democratic convention in 1890; graduated from Cumberland University Law School in 1891; admitted to the bar the same year and practiced in Celina, Tennessee; member of the state House of Representatives 1893—1897; served in Cuba as captain, Fourth Regiment, Tennessee Volunteer Infantry, in 1898; resumed the practice of law; judge of the Fifth Judicial Circuit of Tennessee 1903—1907; Representative from Tennessee 1907—1921 and 1923—1931; married Rose Frances (Witz) Whitney in 1917; chairman of the Democratic National Committee 1921—1924; Senator from Tennessee 1931—1933; commissioned Secretary of State in President Roosevelt's Cabinet March 4, 1933, entered upon his duties the same day, and served until November 30, 1944; as Secretary of State, sponsored a reciprocal-trade program, was chairman of American delegations to numerous international conferences, and was United States delegate to the Moscow Conference in 1943; appointed a delegate to the United Nations Conference at San Francisco in 1945; awarded the Nobel Peace Prize the same year; retired from public life; died at the Naval Hospital, Bethesda, Maryland, July 23, 1955.

Edward Morris Murray, commander, U.S.N.R., was born in Magnolia, Massachusetts, August 7, 1902; died at the United States Naval Air Station, Miami, Florida, April 23, 1946. His portrait of Cordell Hull was painted from life in the Old State Department Building (Executive Office Building) in 1943 while (then) Lieutenant Commander Murray was on duty in the Navy. The portrait was in the possession of Mr. and Mrs. Hull until 1949, when it was sent to the National Gallery of Art, where three copies of it were painted. It was received in the Department of State from the National Gallery on July 22, 1949. Inscription: "E Murray 1943." Size 47¼ by 37¼ inches.

Edward Reilly Stettinius, Jr.

Edward Reilly Stettinius, Jr.

EDWARD REILLY STETTINIUS, Jr., was born in Chicago, Illinois, October 22, 1900; attended the University of Virginia 1919–1924; married Virginia Gordon Wallace in 1926; associated with General Motors Corporation 1926–1934, becoming a vice president in 1931; associated with United States Steel Corporation 1934–1940, becoming chairman of the board of directors in 1938; chairman of the War Resources Board in 1939; member of the advisory committee to the Council of National Defense in 1940; chairman of the Priorities Board and director of the Priorities Division of the Office of Production Management in 1941; Lend-Lease Administrator, special assistant to the President, and a member of the Canadian-American Joint Defense Production Committee 1941–1943; member of the Board of Economic Warfare 1942–1943; Under Secretary of State 1943–1944; commissioned Secretary of State in President Roosevelt's Cabinet November 30, 1944, entered upon his duties December 1, 1944, continued in office under President Truman, and served until June 27, 1945; as Secretary of State, accompanied President Roosevelt to the Yalta Conference in 1945, and was chairman of the United States delegation to the United Nations Conference at San Francisco the same year; was United States representative to the United Nations 1945–1946; rector of the University of Virginia 1946–1949; died in Greenwich, Connecticut, October 31, 1949.

Jes Wilhelm Schlaikjer was born in New York City September 22, 1897. His portrait of Edward R. Stettinius, Jr., which was painted from photographs after Mr. Stettinius' death, was purchased by the Department of State from Mr. Schlaikjer on October 17, 1950. Inscription: "Schlaikjer N.A." Size: 29½ by 24½ inches.

James Francis Byrnes

ARTIST Dickinson

James Francis Byrnes

JAMES FRANCIS BYRNES was born in Charleston, South Carolina, May 2, 1879; attended public schools; official court reporter 1900–1908; admitted to the bar in 1903 and practiced in Aiken, South Carolina; editor of the Aiken *Journal and Review* 1903–1907; married Maude Perkins Busch in 1906; solicitor for the Second Circuit of the State 1908–1910; Representative from South Carolina 1911–1925; delegate to all the Democratic national conventions from 1920 to 1940; practiced law in Spartanburg, South Carolina, 1925–1931; Senator from South Carolina 1931–1941; Associate Justice of the United States Supreme Court 1941–1942; director of the Office of Economic Stabilization 1942–1943; director of the Office of War Mobilization and Reconversion 1943–1945; accompanied President Roosevelt to the Yalta Conference in 1945; commissioned Secretary of State in President Truman's Cabinet July 2, 1945, entered upon his duties July 3, 1945, and served until January 21, 1947; as Secretary of State, accompanied President Truman to the Potsdam Conference in 1945, was United States member of the Council of Foreign Ministers at London in 1945 and at Paris and at New York City in 1946, and represented the United States at the Paris Peace Conference in 1946; practiced law in Washington, D.C., 1947–1950; Governor of South Carolina 1951–1955; died in Columbia, South Carolina, April 9, 1972.

Sidney Edward Dickinson was born in Wallingford, Connecticut, November 28, 1890. His portrait of James F. Byrnes, which was painted from life in 1951, was purchased by the Department of State from Mr. Dickinson on June 11, 1951. Inscription: "Sidney E. Dickinson 1951." Size: 29½ by 24½ inches.

George Catlett Marshall

ARTIST Wi

George Catlett Marshall

GEORGE CATLETT MARSHALL was born in Uniontown, Pennsylvania, December 31, 1880; graduated from Virginia Military Institute in 1901; married Elizabeth Carter Coles in 1902 (died 1927); served in the United States Army 1901–1945, attaining the rank of general of the Army; saw overseas service in World War I; married Katherine Boyce (Tupper) Brown in 1930; Chief of Staff of the Army 1939–1945; participated in the various World War II conferences of President Roosevelt with Prime Minister Churchill and with Marshal Stalin and Generalissimo Chiang Kai-shek; accompanied President Truman to the Potsdam Conference in 1945; special representative of the President to China with the rank of Ambassador 1945–1947; commissioned Secretary of State in President Truman's Cabinet January 8, 1947, entered upon his duties January 21, 1947, and served until January 20, 1949; as Secretary of State, was United States member of the Council of Foreign Ministers at Moscow and at London in 1947, and put forward the "Marshall Plan" for European economic recovery the same year; president of the American National Red Cross 1949–1950; Secretary of Defense 1950–1951; retired from public life; died in Washington, D.C., October 16, 1959.

J. Anthony Wills was born in Berwyn, Pennsylvania, June 13, 1912. Mr. Wills painted five portraits of George C. Marshall. Mrs. Marshall owns one; the others are in the collections of West Point, the National Portrait Gallery, and a private corporation. This portrait, painted from life, was purchased by the Department of State from Mr. Wills on November 7, 1949. Inscription: "J. Anthony Wills." Size: 29½ by 24½ inches.

Dean Gooderham Acheson

ARTIST Cox

Dean Gooderham Acheson

DEAN GOODERHAM ACHESON was born in Middletown, Connecticut, April 11, 1893; graduated from Yale University in 1915 and from Harvard Law School in 1918; married Alice Stanley in 1917; an ensign in the United States Navy 1918—1919; served as private secretary to Louis D. Brandeis, Associate Justice of the United States Supreme Court, 1919—1921; admitted to the bar and practiced in Washington, D.C., 1921—1933 and 1934—1941; Under Secretary of the Treasury in 1933; Assistant Secretary of State 1941—1945 and Under Secretary of State 1945—1947; resumed the practice of law; appointed by the President a member of the Commission on Organization of the Executive Branch of the Government in 1947; chairman of the American section of the Permanent Joint Defense Board 1947—1948; commissioned Secretary of State in President Truman's Cabinet January 19, 1949, entered upon his duties January 21, 1949, and served until January 20, 1953; as Secretary of State, was the United States member of the Council of Foreign Ministers at Paris in 1949, participated in the negotiation and signing of the North Atlantic Treaty of 1949, and served as chairman of the third session of the North Atlantic Council at Washington in 1950; resumed the practice of law; died in Sandy Spring, Maryland, October 12, 1971.

Gardner Cox was born in Holyoke, Massachusetts, January 22, 1906. His portrait of Dean Acheson, which was painted from life, was purchased by the Department of State from Mr. Cox on January 13, 1950. Inscription: "Gardner Cox 1950." Size: 34¼ by 24¼ inches.

John Foster Dulles

John Foster Dulles

JOHN FOSTER DULLES was born in Washington, D.C., February 25, 1888; graduated from Princeton University in 1908; attended the Sorbonne 1908—1909 and George Washington University Law School 1910—1911; practiced law in New York City 1911—1917; married Janet Pomeroy Avery in 1912; served in the United States Army 1917—1918, attaining the rank of major; resumed the practice of law; adviser to President Wilson at the Paris Peace Conference and a member of the Reparations Commission and Supreme Economic Council in 1919; delegate to the Berlin Debt Conferences in 1933, to the United Nations Conference at San Francisco in 1945, and to the United Nations General Assembly in 1946, 1947, 1948, and 1950; interim Senator from New York in 1949; consultant to the Secretary of State in 1950; special representative of the President, with the rank of Ambassador, to negotiate the Japanese peace treaty 1950—1951; commissioned Secretary of State in President Eisenhower's Cabinet January 21, 1953, entered upon his duties the same day, and served until April 22, 1959; during his six-year tenure he made some 60 foreign trips and journeyed a total of almost half a million miles; instrumental in expanding the free world alliance system; died in Washington, D.C., May 24, 1959.

Robert Brackman was born in Odessa, Russia, September 25, 1898; came to the United States in 1908 and was naturalized in 1926. His portrait of John Foster Dulles, which was painted from life in Washington, was done under contract between the Department and Mr. Brackman dated June 23, 1954, and was paid for on March 2, 1955. Inscription: "Brackman." An inscription on the back of the canvas reads: "Portrait of John Foster Dulles, Secretary of State. Painted in Washington, D.C., by Robert Brackman, N.A., 1954." Size: 44 by 34 inches (stretcher measurements).

Christian Archibald Herter

ARTIST Murray

Christian Archibald Herter

CHRISTIAN ARCHIBALD HERTER was born in Paris, France, March 28, 1895; graduated from Harvard in 1915; attaché to U.S. Embassy in Berlin 1916—1917 and for two months in charge of U.S. legation in Brussels; married Mary Caroline Pratt in 1917; served in the Department of State from 1917—1919; secretary, U.S. Commission to Negotiate Peace, Paris 1918—1919; personal assistant to Secretary of Commerce Herbert Hoover 1919—1924; executive secretary of the European Relief Council 1920—1921; newspaper editor and associate editor 1924—1936; lecturer, Harvard University 1929—1930; served in the Massachusetts House of Representatives 1931—1943 and as Speaker of that body 1939—1943; Representative to the U.S. Congress 1943—1953 and head of a House select committee that helped pave the way for the Marshall Plan; Governor of Massachusetts from 1953 to 1957; served as Under Secretary of State 1957—1959 and commissioned Secretary of State in President Eisenhower's Cabinet on April 21, 1959, entered upon his duties April 22, 1959, and served until January 20, 1961; served as a trade negotiator in the administrations of John F. Kennedy and Lyndon B. Johnson; died in Washington, D.C., December 30, 1966.

Albert Murray was born in Emporia, Kansas, December 29, 1906.
His portrait of Christian A. Herter was painted from life and from
photographic study in 1960. Inscription: "Albert Murray 1960."
Size: 30 by 24½ inches.

Dean Rusk

ARTIST Cox

Dean Rusk

DEAN DAVID RUSK was born in Cherokee County, Georgia, February 9, 1909; graduated from Davidson College in 1931; as a Rhodes Scholar studied at St. John's College, Oxford University 1931—1934; from 1934 to 1940 on the faculty of Mills College, Oakland, California and appointed Dean of Faculty in 1938; married Virginia Foisie in 1937; attained the rank of colonel during World War II and served as the deputy chief of staff for the China-Burma-India theater; assistant chief of the Department of State's Division of International Security Affairs in 1946; special assistant to the Secretary of War 1946; from 1947 to 1949 served in the Department of State as director of the Office of Special Political Affairs which later became the Office of United Nations Affairs; in 1949 appointed Deputy Under Secretary of State; in 1950 appointed Assistant Secretary of State for Far Eastern Affairs; president of the Rockefeller Foundation 1952—1961; commissioned Secretary of State in President Kennedy's Cabinet on January 21, 1961, entered upon his duties the same day, continued in office under President Johnson, and served until January 20, 1969; helped deal with such problems as the Cuban Missile Crisis, the 1967 Arab-Israeli war, the Dominican Republic intervention, the "Pueblo" incident, the closure of the border between East and West Berlin, and especially the Vietnam war; professor of international law at the University of Georgia 1969 to the present.

Gardner Cox also painted the Department's portrait of Dean Acheson (*q.v.*). The Rusk portrait was painted in 1964. Inscription: "Gardner Cox 1964." Size: 49½ by 34½ inches.

William Pierce Rogers

ARTIST Gittins

William Pierce Rogers

WILLIAM PIERCE ROGERS was born in Norfolk, New York, on June 23, 1913; graduated from Colgate University in 1934 and earned a law degree from Cornell University in 1937; married Adele Langston in 1936; Assistant District Attorney of New York County 1938—1942 and 1946—1947; served in U.S. Navy 1942—1946; counsel and chief counsel to the U.S. Senate Special Committee to Investigate the National Defense Program 1947—1948; chief counsel to the Senate Investigations Subcommittee of the Executive Expenditures Committee 1948—1950; practiced law 1950—53; Deputy Attorney General 1953—1957; Attorney General 1957—1961; served as member of the U.S. delegation to the U.N. 20th General Assembly in 1965; member of the President's National Commission on Law Enforcement and Administration of Justice 1965—1967; U.S. representative to the United Nations in 1967; commissioned Secretary of State in President Nixon's Cabinet on January 21, 1969, entered upon duties January 22, 1969, and served until September 3, 1973; promoted a cease-fire in the Middle East in 1970 which lasted until the 1973 war; dealt with problems of security and cooperation in Europe; signed the Vietnam peace agreement; returned to the practice of law; received the Presidential Medal of Freedom October 15, 1973.

Alvin Gittins was born in England in 1922 and studied at the Kidderminster School of Arts and Crafts; came to the United States in 1946. Professor of Art at the University of Utah. His portrait of William Rogers was painted in 1974. Inscription: "Gittins 74." Size: 45½ by 33½ inches.

Henry Alfred Kissinger

Henry Alfred Kissinger

HENRY ALFRED KISSINGER was born in Fürth, Germany, on May 27, 1923; emigrated to the United States in 1938; served in the U.S. Army in World War II; married Anne Fleischer in 1949—divorced in 1964; married Nancy Maginnes in 1974; earned his B.A. in 1950, M.A. in 1952, and Ph.D. in 1954 at Harvard University and was a member of the faculty from 1954 to 1971; consultant on foreign policy in the Kennedy and Johnson administrations; adviser to Governor Nelson Rockefeller of New York; named Assistant for National Security Affairs by President Nixon in 1968; in this position his many activities included participation in the 1972 presidential visit to the People's Republic of China and in the negotiations leading to the Vietnam peace agreement; commissioned Secretary of State in President Nixon's Cabinet on September 21, 1973, entered upon duties on September 22, 1973, continued in office under President Ford, and served until January 20, 1977; among other accomplishments as Secretary of State, was instrumental in the signing of cease-fire agreements by Israel with Egypt and Syria in 1973; promoted policy of detente with Soviet Union, which included the signing of trade and arms agreements; dealt with problems of energy and economic cooperation; awarded Nobel Peace Prize in 1973; lecturer and consultant on foreign affairs.

Cyrus Roberts Vance

Cyrus Roberts Vance

CYRUS ROBERTS VANCE was born in Clarkburg, West Virginia, on March 27, 1917; graduated from Yale University in 1939 and Yale University Law School in 1942; served in the U.S. Navy during World War II; married Grace Sloane in 1947; practiced law in New York City, 1947—1960 and 1967—1977; consulting counsel for the Senate Special Committee on Space and Astronautics in 1958; General Counsel for the Department of Defense 1961—1962; Secretary of the Army 1962—1964 and Deputy Secretary of Defense 1964—1967; President's special representative investigating the Detroit civil disturbances in 1967; served as special representative of the President in the Cyprus crisis in 1967; in 1968 was special representative of the President in Korea; negotiator at the Paris Peace Conference on Vietnam 1968—1969; commissioned Secretary of State in President Carter's Cabinet on January 23, 1977, and entered upon his duties the same day.

Appendix A

SECRETARIES OF STATE AD INTERIM

Persons who perform the duties of Secretary of State during a period when there is no Secretary of State in office—during a period, that is, between the retirement, dismissal, or death of one Secretary of State and his successor's entry upon the duties of the office—are usually referred to collectively as Secretaries of State ad interim. There is no statutory provision specifying the title to be used in these circumstances. Since Jefferson took office as the first Secretary of State there have been thirty-one periods of service of Secretaries of State ad interim. In the case of six of these periods the persons who served as Secretary ad interim were ones who, at some other time or times, held formal commissions as Secretary of State. These persons were Timothy Pickering, John Marshall (two periods), James Monroe, Abel P. Upshur, and Robert Lansing. Listed below are the persons who have acted as Secretary of State when that office was vacant, with the following information on each: name, legal residence, government position held at the time (if any), title used while acting as Secretary of State (if known), and dates during which each person was in charge of the Department of State.

Timothy Pickering, of Pennsylvania (Secretary of War)
    Executing the office of Secretary of State August 20—December 9, 1795.
Charles Lee, of Virginia (Attorney General)
    Executing the office of Secretary of State, and also Secretary of State ad interim May 13—June 5, 1800.
John Marshall, of Virginia (Chief Justice of the United States)
    Acting as Secretary of State February 4—March 4, 1801.
Levi Lincoln, of Massachusetts (Attorney General)
    Acting as Secretary of State March 5—May 1, 1801.
James Monroe, of Virginia (Secretary of War)
    Acting Secretary of State October 1, 1814—February 28, 1815.
John Graham, of Virginia (Chief Clerk)
    March 4—9, 1817.
Richard Rush, of Pennsylvania (Attorney General)
    Acting Secretary of State March 10—September 22, 1817.
Daniel Brent, of Virginia (Chief Clerk)
    March 4—7, 1825.
James A. Hamilton, of New York
    Acting Secretary of State March 4—27, 1829.

Jacob L. Martin, of North Carolina (Chief Clerk)
  Acting Secretary of State March 4—5, 1841.
Hugh S. Legaré, of South Carolina (Attorney General)
  Secretary of State ad interim May 9—June 20, 1843.
William S. Derrick, of Pennsylvania (Chief Clerk)
  Acting Secretary of State June 21—23, 1843.
Abel P. Upshur, of Virginia (Secretary of the Navy)
  Secretary of State ad interim June 24—July 23, 1843.
John Nelson, of Maryland (Attorney General)
  Secretary of State ad interim February 29—March 31, 1844.
Charles M. Conrad, of Louisiana (Secretary of War)
  Acting Secretary of State October 25—November 5, 1852.
William Hunter Jr., of Rhode Island (Chief Clerk)
  Acting Secretary of State March 4—7, 1853, and December 15—16, 1860.
William F. Wharton, of Massachusetts (Assistant Secretary)
  Acting Secretary of State June 4—29, 1892, and February 24—March 6, 1893.
Edwin F. Uhl, of Michigan (Assistant Secretary)
  Acting Secretary of State May 28—June 9, 1895.
Alvey A. Adee, of the District of Columbia (Second Assistant Secretary)
  Acting Secretary of State September 17—29, 1898.
Francis B. Loomis, of Ohio (Assistant Secretary)
  July 1—18, 1905.
Robert Lansing, of New York (Counselor)
  Secretary of State ad interim June 9—23, 1915.
Frank Lyon Polk, of New York (Under Secretary)
  Acting Secretary of State February 14—March 14, 1920.
Joseph C. Grew, of New Hampshire (Under Secretary)
  Acting Secretary of State June 28—July 3, 1945.
H. Freeman Matthews, of Maryland (Deputy Under Secretary)
  Secretary of State ad interim January 20—21, 1953.
Livingston T. Merchant, of the District of Columbia (Under Secretary for Political Affairs)
  Secretary of State ad interim January 20—21, 1961.
Charles E. Bohlen, of the District of Columbia (Deputy Under Secretary for Political Affairs)
  Acting Secretary of State January 20—22, 1969.
Kenneth Rush, of New York (Deputy Secretary)
  Acting Secretary of State September 3—22, 1973.
Philip C. Habib, of New York (Under Secretary for Political Affairs)
  Secretary of State ad interim January 20—23, 1977.

For a list in chronological order of all the Secretaries of State and Secretaries of State ad interim, see appendix B.

Appendix B

Chronological List of Presidents of the United States, Secretaries for Foreign Affairs, Secretaries of State, and Secretaries of State Ad Interim[1]

President	Secretary of State[2]
George Washington, of Virginia, April 30, 1789—March 4, 1797.	Robert R. Livingston, of New York, Secretary for Foreign Affairs under the Continental Congress from October 20, 1781 to June 4, 1783. The President of the Continental Congress acted as Secretary for Foreign Affairs ad interim from June 4, 1783 to March 2, 1784, when Congress elected Henry Remsen, Jr., who was undersecretary in the office for foreign affairs, to take charge of the office until December 21, 1784.
	John Jay, of New York, Secretary for Foreign Affairs under the Continental Congress from December 21, 1784; continued unofficially to superintend the Department of State, after the Constitution went into effect, until Jefferson took office as Secretary of State.
	Thomas Jefferson, of Virginia. Commissioned September 26, 1789; entered upon duties March 22, 1790; retired December 31, 1793.
	Edmund Randolph, of Virginia. Commissioned and entered upon duties January 2, 1794; retired August 20, 1795.
	Timothy Pickering, of Pennsylvania (Secretary of War). Executing the office of Secretary of State August 20—December 9, 1795; commissioned Secretary of State and entered upon duties December 10, 1795.
John Adams, of Massachusetts, March 4, 1797—March 4, 1801.	Timothy Pickering continued from preceding administration; retired May 12, 1800.
	Charles Lee, of Virginia (Attorney General). Executing the office of Secretary of State, and also ad interim May 13—June 5, 1800.
	John Marshall, of Virginia. Commissioned May 13, 1800; entered upon duties June 6, 1800; retired February 4, 1801; (Chief Justice of the United States) acting February 4—March 3, 1801.
Thomas Jefferson, of Virginia, March 4, 1801—March 4, 1809.	John Marshall, of Virginia (Chief Justice). Acting March 4, 1801.
	Levi Lincoln, of Massachusetts (Attorney General). Acting March 5—May 1, 1801.

President	Secretary of State
James Madison, of Virginia. March 4, 1809—March 4, 1817.	**James Madison**, of Virginia. Commissioned March 5, 1801; entered upon duties May 2, 1801; retired March 3, 1809. [No Secretary of State or Acting Secretary of State, March 4–5, 1809.] **Robert Smith**, of Maryland. Commissioned and entered upon duties March 6, 1809; retired April 1, 1811. **James Monroe**, of Virginia. Commissioned (recess of the Senate) April 2, 1811; entered upon duties April 6, 1811; recommissioned November 26, 1811; retired September 30, 1814; (Secretary of War) acting October 1, 1814—February 28, 1815; commissioned Secretary of State and entered upon duties February 28, 1815; retired March 3, 1817.
James Monroe, of Virginia March 4, 1817—March 4, 1825.	**John Graham**, of Virginia (Chief Clerk). March 4–9, 1817.[3] **Richard Rush**, of Pennsylvania (Attorney General). Acting March 10—September 22, 1817. **John Quincy Adams**, of Massachusetts. Commissioned March 5, 1817; entered upon duties September 22, 1817; retired March 3, 1825.
John Quincy Adams, of Massachusetts. March 4, 1825—March 4, 1829	**Daniel Brent**, of Virginia (Chief Clerk). March 4–7, 1825.[3] **Henry Clay**, of Kentucky. Commissioned and entered upon duties March 7, 1825; retired March 3, 1829.
Andrew Jackson, of Tennessee, March 4, 1829—March 4, 1837.	**James A. Hamilton**, of New York. Acting March 4–27, 1829. **Martin Van Buren**, of New York. Commissioned March 6, 1829; entered upon duties March 28, 1829; retired May 23, 1831. **Edward Livingston**, of Louisiana. Commissioned (recess of the Senate) and entered upon duties May 24, 1831; recommissioned January 12, 1832; retired May 29, 1833. **Louis McLane**, of Delaware. Commissioned (recess of the Senate) and entered upon duties May 29, 1833; retired June 30, 1834. **John Forsyth**, of Georgia. Commissioned June 27, 1834; entered upon duties July 1, 1834.
Martin Van Buren, of New York, March 4, 1837—March 4, 1841.	**John Forsyth** continued from preceding administration; retired March 3, 1841.
William Henry Harrison, of Ohio, March 4—April 4, 1841.	**Jacob L. Martin**, of North Carolina (Chief Clerk). Acting March 4–5, 1841. **Daniel Webster**, of Massachusetts. Commissioned March 5, 1841; entered upon duties March 6, 1841.

See footnotes at end of table.

President—Continued	Secretary of State—Continued
John Tyler, of Virginia, April 6, 1841–March 4, 1845.	Daniel Webster continued from preceding administration; retired May 8, 1843.
	Hugh S. Legaré, of South Carolina (Attorney General). Ad interim May 9–June 20, 1843 (died).
	William S. Derrick, of Pennsylvania (Chief Clerk). Acting June 21–23, 1843.
	Abel P. Upshur, of Virginia (Secretary of the Navy). Ad interim June 24–July 23, 1843; commissioned Secretary of State (recess of the Senate) and entered upon duties July 24, 1843; recommissioned January 2, 1844; died February 28, 1844.
	John Nelson, of Maryland (Attorney General). Ad interim February 29–March 31, 1844.
	John C. Calhoun, of South Carolina. Commissioned March 6, 1844; entered upon duties April 1, 1844.
James K. Polk, of Tennessee, March 4, 1845–March 4, 1849.	John C. Calhoun continued from preceding administration; retired March 10, 1845.
	James Buchanan, of Pennsylvania. Commissioned March 6, 1845; entered upon duties March 10, 1845.
Zachary Taylor, of Louisiana, March 5,[4] 1849–July 9, 1850.	James Buchanan continued from preceding administration; retired March 7, 1849.
	John M. Clayton, of Delaware. Commissioned March 7, 1849; entered upon duties March 8, 1849.
Millard Fillmore, of New York, July 10, 1850–March 4, 1853.	John M. Clayton continued from preceding administration; retired July 22, 1850.
	Daniel Webster, of Massachusetts. Commissioned July 22, 1850; entered upon duties July 23, 1850; died October 24, 1852.
	Charles M. Conrad, of Louisiana (Secretary of War). Acting October 25–November 5, 1852.
	Edward Everett, of Massachusetts. Commissioned (recess of the Senate) and entered upon duties November 6, 1852; recommissioned December 9, 1852; retired March 3, 1853.
Franklin Pierce, of New Hampshire, March 4, 1853–March 4, 1857.	William Hunter, Jr., of Rhode Island (Chief Clerk). Acting March 4–7, 1853.
	William L. Marcy, of New York. Commissioned March 7, 1853; entered upon duties March 8, 1853.

President	Secretary of State
James Buchanan, of Pennsylvania. March 4, 1857—March 4, 1861.	William L. Marcy continued from preceding administration; retired March 6, 1857.
	Lewis Cass, of Michigan. Commissioned and entered upon duties March 6, 1857; retired December 14, 1860.
	William Hunter, Jr., of Rhode Island (Chief Clerk). Acting December 15–16, 1860.
	Jeremiah S. Black, of Pennsylvania. Commissioned and entered upon duties December 17, 1860.
Abraham Lincoln, of Illinois, March 4, 1861—April 15, 1865.	Jeremiah S. Black continued from preceding administration; retired March 5, 1861.
	William H. Seward, of New York. Commissioned March 5, 1861; entered upon duties March 6, 1861.
Andrew Johnson, of Tennessee, April 15, 1865—March 4, 1869.	William H. Seward continued from preceding administration; retired March 4, 1869.
Ulysses S. Grant, of Illinois, March 4, 1869—March 4, 1877.	Elihu B. Washburne, of Illinois. Commissioned and entered upon duties March 5, 1869; retired March 16, 1869.
	Hamilton Fish, of New York. Commissioned March 11, 1869; entered upon duties March 17, 1869; recommissioned March 17, 1873.
Rutherford B. Hayes, of Ohio, March 4,⁵ 1877—March 4, 1881.	Hamilton Fish continued from preceding administration; retired March 12, 1877.
	William M. Evarts, of New York. Commissioned and entered upon duties March 12, 1877.
James A. Garfield, of Ohio, March 4—September 19, 1881.	William M. Evarts continued from preceding administration; retired March 7, 1881.
	James G. Blaine, of Maine. Commissioned March 5, 1881; entered upon duties March 7, 1881.
Chester A. Arthur, of New York, September 20, 1881—March 4, 1885.	James G. Blaine continued from preceding administration; retired December 19, 1881.
	Frederick T. Frelinghuysen, of New Jersey. Commissioned December 12, 1881; entered upon duties December 19, 1881.
Grover Cleveland, of New York, March 4, 1885—March 4, 1889.	Frederick T. Frelinghuysen continued from preceding administration; retired March 6, 1885.
	Thomas F. Bayard, of Delaware. Commissioned March 6, 1885; entered upon duties March 7, 1885.

See footnotes at end of table.

President—Continued	Secretary of State—Continued
Benjamin Harrison, of Indiana, March 4, 1889—March 4, 1893.	**Thomas F. Bayard** continued from preceding administration; retired March 6, 1889.
	James G. Blaine, of Maine. Commissioned March 5, 1889; entered upon duties March 7, 1889; retired June 4, 1892.
	William F. Wharton, of Massachusetts (Assistant Secretary). Acting June 4—29, 1892.
	John W. Foster, of Indiana. Commissioned and entered upon duties June 29, 1892; retired February 23, 1893.
	William F. Wharton, of Massachusetts (Assistant Secretary). Acting February 24, 1893, to close of administration.
Grover Cleveland, of New York, March 4, 1893—March 4, 1897.	**William F. Wharton** continued, acting, from preceding administration to March 6, 1893.
	Walter Q. Gresham, of Illinois. Commissioned March 6, 1893; entered upon duties March 7, 1893; died May 28, 1895.
	Edwin F. Uhl, of Michigan (Assistant Secretary). Acting May 28—June 9, 1895.
	Richard Olney, of Massachusetts. Commissioned (recess of the Senate) June 8, 1895; entered upon duties June 10, 1895; recommissioned December 3, 1895.
William McKinley, of Ohio, March 4, 1897—September 14, 1901.	**Richard Olney** continued from preceding administration; retired March 5, 1897.
	John Sherman, of Ohio. Commissioned March 5, 1897; entered upon duties March 6, 1897; retired April 27, 1898.
	William R. Day, of Ohio. Commissioned April 26, 1898; entered upon duties April 28, 1898; retired September 16, 1898.
	Alvey A. Adee, of the District of Columbia (Second Assistant Secretary). Acting September 17—29, 1898.
	John Hay, of the District of Columbia. Commissioned (recess of the Senate) September 20, 1898; entered upon duties September 30, 1898; recommissioned December 7, 1898, and March 5, 1901.
Theodore Roosevelt, of New York, September 14, 1901—March 4, 1909.	**John Hay** continued from preceding administration; recommissioned March 6, 1905; died July 1, 1905.
	Francis B. Loomis, of Ohio (Assistant Secretary). July 1—18, 1905.[3]
	Elihu Root, of New York. Commissioned (recess of the Senate) July 7, 1905; entered upon duties July 19, 1905; recommissioned December 6, 1905; retired January 27, 1909.

Robert Bacon, of New York. Commissioned and entered upon duties January 27, 1909.

Robert Bacon continued from preceding administration; retired March 5, 1909.

William H. Taft, of Ohio,
March 4, 1909–March 4, 1913.

Philander C. Knox, of Pennsylvania. Commissioned March 5, 1909; entered upon duties March 6, 1909.

Philander C. Knox continued from preceding administration; retired March 5, 1913.

Woodrow Wilson, of New Jersey,
March 4, 1913–March 4, 1921.

William Jennings Bryan, of Nebraska. Commissioned and entered upon duties March 5, 1913; retired June 9, 1915.

Robert Lansing, of New York (Counselor). Ad interim June 9–23, 1915; commissioned (recess of the Senate) June 23, 1915; entered upon duties June 24, 1915; recommissioned December 13, 1915; retired February 13, 1920.

Frank Lyon Polk, of New York (Under Secretary). Acting February 14–March 14, 1920.

[No Secretary of State or Acting Secretary of State, March 15–21, 1920.[6]]

Bainbridge Colby, of New York. Commissioned March 22, 1920; entered upon duties March 23, 1920; retired March 4, 1921.

Charles E. Hughes, of New York. Commissioned March 4, 1921; entered upon duties March 5, 1921.

Warren G. Harding, of Ohio,
March 4, 1921–August 2, 1923.

Calvin Coolidge, of Massachusetts,
August 3, 1923–March 4, 1929.

Charles E. Hughes continued from preceding administration; retired March 4, 1925.

Frank B. Kellogg, of Minnesota. Commissioned February 16, 1925; entered upon duties March 5, 1925.

Herbert C. Hoover, of California,
March 4, 1929–March 4, 1933.

Frank B. Kellogg continued from preceding administration; retired March 28, 1929.

Henry L. Stimson, of New York. Commissioned March 5, 1929; entered upon duties March 28, 1929; retired March 4, 1933.

Franklin D. Roosevelt, of New York,
March 4, 1933–April 12, 1945.

Cordell Hull, of Tennessee. Commissioned and entered upon duties March 4, 1933; retired November 30, 1944.

Edward R. Stettinius, Jr., of Virginia. Commissioned November 30, 1944; entered upon duties December 1, 1944.

See footnotes at end of table.

President—Continued	Secretary of State—Continued
Harry S. Truman, of Missouri, April 12, 1945–January 20, 1953.	Edward R. Stettinius, Jr., continued from preceding administration; retired June 27, 1945.
	Joseph C. Grew, of New Hampshire (Under Secretary). Acting June 28–July 3, 1945.
	James F. Byrnes, of South Carolina. Commissioned July 2, 1945; entered upon duties July 3, 1945; retired January 21, 1947.
	George C. Marshall, of Pennsylvania. Commissioned January 8, 1947; entered upon duties January 21, 1947; retired January 20, 1949.
	Dean Acheson, of Maryland. Commissioned January 19, 1949; entered upon duties January 21, 1949; retired January 20, 1953.
Dwight D. Eisenhower, of New York, January 20, 1953–January 20, 1961.	H. Freeman Matthews, of Maryland (Deputy Under Secretary). Ad interim January 20–21, 1953.
	John Foster Dulles, of New York. Commissioned and entered upon duties January 21, 1953; retired April 22, 1959.
	Christian A. Herter, of Massachusetts. Commissioned April 21, 1959; entered upon duties April 22, 1959; retired January 20, 1961.
John F. Kennedy, of Massachusetts, January 20, 1961–November 22, 1963.	Livingston T. Merchant, of the District of Columbia (Under Secretary for Political Affairs). Ad interim January 20–21, 1961.
	Dean Rusk, of New York. Commissioned and entered upon duties January 21, 1961.
Lyndon B. Johnson, of Texas, November 22, 1963–January 20, 1969.	Dean Rusk, continued from preceding administration; retired January 20, 1969.
Richard M. Nixon, of California, January 20, 1969–August 9, 1974.	Charles E. Bohlen, of the District of Columbia (Deputy Under Secretary for Political Affairs). Acting January 20–22, 1969.
	William P. Rogers, of Maryland. Commissioned January 21, 1969; entered upon duties January 22, 1969; retired September 3, 1973.
	Kenneth Rush, of New York (Deputy Secretary of State). Acting September 3–22, 1973.
	Henry A. Kissinger, of the District of Columbia. Commissioned September 21, 1973; entered upon duties September 22, 1973.

Gerald R. Ford, of Michigan, August 9, 1974–January 20, 1977.

Jimmy Carter, of Georgia, January 20, 1977–

Henry A. Kissinger, continued from preceding administration; retired January 20, 1977.

Philip C. Habib, of New York (Under Secretary for Political Affairs). Ad interim January 20–23, 1977.

Cyrus R. Vance, of New York. Commissioned and entered upon duties January 23, 1977.

---

[1] Secretary of State ad interim is used here to include all persons who performed as Secretary of State when there was no Secretary of State in office. They may have been given other titles, such as Acting Secretary of State.

[2] The title "Secretary of State" dates from September 15, 1789.

[3] Title not known.

[4] March 4, 1849, fell on Sunday.

[5] President-elect Hayes was entertained March 3, 1877, at the White House as the guest of President Grant, where he took the oath privately. On Monday, March 5, he took the oath publicly.

[6] From an opinion of the Solicitor of the Department of State.

☆ U. S. GOVERNMENT PRINTING OFFICE : 1978 O - 275-388